ENTERTAINING DECEPTION

The New Apostolic Reformation Coming To A Calvary Chapel Near You

Dr. David Newton

INSIGHTS PUBLISHING HOUSE

SANTA BARBARA ⓘ CALIFORNIA

ISBN: 978-1-5323-4029-1

Insights Publishing House is committed to examining the ever-changing contemporary issues in the church through the never-changing lens of sound Biblical doctrine.

ⓘ   ⓘ   ⓘ

Contact David Newton directly for him to speak to your church or ministry group: InsightsNewton@gmail.com

Other resources at: www.InsightsNewtonNAR.org

CONTENTS

ACKNOWLEDGEMENTS

First, I'd like to thank the many close friends and family members who strongly encouraged me to go through all my research files and teaching notes to turn those into this book. I also want to thank the faithful prayer and financial partners who helped get this endeavor from conceptual idea to finished product. Thanks to Jenny Newton Designs for the cover art and the book's new website. Finally, none of this would be possible if not for Pastor Chuck's commitment to teach the full counsel of God's Word, verse-by-verse, Genesis to Revelation - holding to his timeless philosophy of ministry and vision for Calvary Chapel.

FOREWORD

Pastor Chuck's 1989 "Philosophy of Ministry at Calvary Chapel" is this. *"The philosophy of Calvary Chapel is to perfect the saints for the work of the ministry and to build up the body of Christ, instructing them in the Word until they come into the unity of the faith and the knowledge of the Son of God, and into a full maturity, unto the stature of the measure of the image of Christ".* During my 40 years as a Calvary Chapel pastor my number one goal has always been to teach God's Word with sound doctrine, so I would equip the saints to do the ministry. When people have a strong foundation in God's Word, they are prepared to do all kinds of service inside and outside the church. They can teach Sunday school or be on a worship team. They can join the prayer team or the women's ministry. They can visit men in prison or do discipleship. They are ready for an Easter outreach or a short-term missions trip.

Pastor Chuck also said this. *"Calvary Chapel believes in teaching the Word of God through the power of the Spirit of God which changes the lives of the people of God; if you have just the Spirit-emphasis with no Word and no foundation in the Word, then you are leading the people into experiences only, which are shallow; if you have just the Word of God without the Spirit, then you are leading people into dead orthodoxy. It takes the power of the Spirit of God to make the changes, but it takes the Word of God to give the substance and to give the foundation. It is that blending of the Word of God and being taught through the power of the Spirit of God that brings the changes in the people".*

This book is timely and so needed because Calvary Chapel's distinctives are being challenged from false teachers and deceptive doctrines coming from the global movement known as the New Apostolic Reformation (NAR). Dr. Dave explains what's going on, and how sound doctrine and strong pastoral care is needed more than ever from Calvary pastors, elders, deacons, worship leaders, and everyone involved in lay-ministries. It's also really important for our young people to be taught the full counsel of God's Word so they are equipped as the next generation to give an answer to these deceptions and false practices. This book is also a great resource for anyone who attends Calvary Chapel each week, so they will know and understand what's happening.

Pastor Chuck introduced me to Dave Newton at the pastor's conference in Costa Mesa in April of 1990. I was all set to move from Kumulani Chapel on Mau'i to be the senior pastor at Calvary Chapel Santa Barbara. Dave would be moving up to Santa Barbara from Orange County that summer. We ministered together for 20 years, so I know first-hand his love for God's Word, and his ability to teach it with integrity and sound doctrine. We both love Calvary Chapel and Pastor Chuck's vision for ministry. There's a great opportunity now for Calvary Chapels everywhere to "strengthen those things that remain", built on the strong foundation of God's Word. And we both agree with Pastor Chuck's summary - *"Calvary Chapel has a biblically sound and balanced understanding of the church, its function in the world, and its total dependence upon the leading and guiding of the Holy Spirit, as it faithfully proclaims the Good News of the cross of Jesus Christ and the hope of salvation through Him only"* - 'for as the rain and the snow come from heaven and do not return without watering the earth, making it bear and sprout, giving seed to the sower and bread to the eater, so will My Word be from My mouth; It will not return to Me empty, without accomplishing what I desire, and without succeeding *in the matter* for which I sent it' [Isaiah 55:10-11]. May this book richly bless you.

- Ricky Ryan
Lahaina on Mau'i

Pastor Ricky moved to Mau'i in 1973 and was the founding pastor of Kumulani Chapel (1980-1990). Pastor Chuck then invited him to be senior pastor at Calvary Chapel Santa Barbara, where he served for 20 years. In 2010 the Lord called him back to Kumulani, where he pastors alongside Greg Laurie with Harvest at Kumulani. He also served on the Calvary Chapel Association Leadership Council from 2012-2016.

INTRODUCTION

This book is written for everyone who attends one of the 1,700 Calvary Chapel churches around the world, with a specific focus intended for pastors, elders, and lay leaders - because a significant and disturbing challenge to the core Biblical principles of Calvary Chapel has been gaining momentum in undermining the sound doctrine upon which the church has stood for more than five decades. *Entertaining Deception.* My intent is for this to be a provocative title - to provoke serious conversations and a detailed examination of how unbiblical deception is at the doorway of the Calvary Chapel movement, and is now subtly (and not so subtly) making its way into all facets of worship, ministries, home groups, and even pastoral teaching. There are two clear perspectives I want to capture with this title. The first is that the false doctrinal deceptions of the contemporary movement commonly referred to as the New Apostolic Reformation (NAR) are deliberately packaged in an *entertaining* form specifically designed to dazzle audiences - delivered in spectacular fashion to support the basis that this is a major movement of God. The second is that an increasing number of pastors and church leaders throughout Calvary Chapels have relaxed their spiritual discernment and passively tolerated the doctrines and practices of the NAR. Letting down their guard, they are now *entertaining* deception on multiple levels within the spiritual life of their churches.

Those caught up in the NAR's deceptive practices typically remark how they were attracted to the *entertaining* aspects of these purported supernatural manifestations. This includes the way they are packaged and promoted, with the overriding message that God is doing a "new" work and taking the church in a whole "new" direction, and they will get to be a central participant in that. They say they want to be a part of the "next big move of God". They earnestly desire more dramatic personal experiences, revelations, signs and wonders, and miracles - always looking for and expecting something bigger, better, deeper, closer, and more fantastic than the prior sensations. It's in this context that the word *"entertaining"* is an adjective to describe the high profile of the deception. But it's also the verb that explains the ways in which many church leaders have let down their spiritual watchfulness and allowed this deception to slowly, subtly, quietly make its way into the church. Many Calvary Chapel pastors, elders, deacons, worship leaders, and lay leaders are literally sitting by doing little or nothing to address, confront, call out, or deal directly with the clearly unbiblical deception of the NAR. This lack of action means they are passively *entertaining* these supposed "new" spiritual revelations and doctrines within worship songs and weekly church services, home Bible studies, pastoral teachings, as well as a wide range of ministries — from high school and college groups, to men's fellowships and discipleship, women's bible studies and retreats, missions trips, married couples, and prayer teams. This exposes a lack of true spiritual leadership, discernment, and wisdom. In many cases, there's no pastoral vigilance overseeing the sheep, as they casually allow deception to slide into the sanctuaries and ministry areas of Calvary Chapels, highlighting my direct question for them, "Why are you *entertaining* this kind of deception within your core mission and ministry?"

Sad to say, many leaders in the contemporary church have acquiesced into a dangerous form of political correctness that avoids altogether the review and doctrinal discernment of questionable practices because it's considered a personal insult to challenge another person's beliefs or individual expression of Christianity. The most common responses include: "Who am I to tell someone else what they can and can't do in the church?" "If this helps the person feel closer to God, can it be wrong?" "Who's to say whether this is really of the Holy Spirit?" "If some good is happening, why be so focused on the negative?" "Maybe it's not quite right, but they're so sincere and have such passion." "If this is what they feel led to do, why should that concern me?" "We all believe in Jesus, right, so let's respect individual preferences". Even more alarming are those leaders who are intentionally integrating this deception into their ministry areas of Calvary Chapel - not passive intrusion, but an active embracing of one or more of these unbiblical practices, deceptive teachings, and false doctrines.

One form of *entertaining* deception refers to the various "new" religious movements, churches, practices, pastors, prophets, and apostles in the NAR who focus on *entertaining* people through their worship content and style, sensational displays in healing rooms and services, dramatic publicly-declared words of knowledge, thrilling prophetic forecasts, or promises to become spiritually superior (elite) through conferences, events, courses, books, and online web postings. These all leverage recycled sensational experiences with an appeal aimed at drawing people into multiple forms of deception. It's enticing, alluring, and offers the opportunity to "feel closer to God". But let me clearly say that having watched their DVDs, online videos and podcasts, listened to their MP3 and CD teachings and testimonies, read their books, magazines, and PDFs, and reviewed their prophecy and apostolic websites, these ALL pursue an *entertaining* angle about what they do, say, and sing. It is aimed at creating (manufacturing) their own unique branding of "one-of-a-kind" spiritual sensationalism with a focus on *entertaining* (drawing in and appealing to) the emotions of the masses. However, it is very sad to not only see, hear, and read these various deceptions, but to spend time talking with people from many

Calvary Chapel churches who have been lured away into these supposedly "new" revelations, movements, music, and special words from God. We have to ask the tough questions: How does this happen? What enticement draws them in so quickly? "Why don't they recognize this deception at the very start? "Do they really not understand that this stuff is false?" and of course, "Why don't they compare this directly to the truths in God's Word?"

For nearly 50 years, Calvary Chapel was a very steady, reliable, and consistent church movement. It developed a highly trusted name, like a seal of confidence, was solid in its foundations, always taught sound doctrine, and had balanced worship and Biblical truth for tens of thousands of people. Pastors faithfully taught God's Word, did not get "weird" during the worship services, and held fast to timeless core Biblical doctrine. Whenever my family was traveling on vacation, or I was out of town on business, it was always nice to find the local Calvary Chapel in another city, knowing that the worship, sermon from God's Word, and fellowship would be something I could rely on - consistent and biblically sound - just like back at our home Calvary Chapel. We used to visit Calvary Chapel Encinitas whenever we were did holidays at my in-laws in north San Diego County, or Horizon when visiting my youngest daughter during her years at San Diego State, or Maranatha Chapel when I was doing graduate research near Scripps Ranch. The wonderful consistency of the sound teaching from God's Word also came through time and again for 30+ years listening on 107.9 KWVE with Pastor Chuck, Jeff Johnson, Raul Ries, Skip Heitzig, Ray Bentley, Dave Rolph, Jon Courson, Steve Mays, Don McClure, Greg Laurie, Ray Stedman, Chuck Missler, Bob Hoekstra, or Mike MacIntosh. The praise and worship music was also always a refreshing balance of beautiful melodies with biblically sound lyrics to focus our hearts and minds entirely on our Lord, His mercy, love, grace, kindness, power, and majesty. So whether we were at Calvary Chapel in San Jose, Escondido, Big Bear, Nice, Irvine, Denver, Ventura, Lyon, Downey, East London, Oxnard, or Paris, we were never concerned about the worship, the service, or the pastor's teaching being doctrinally sound.

However, the last several years have seen a dramatic increase in the ways that false doctrines, deceptive worship, aberrant prayer, unbiblical counseling, weird practices, and "new" directions from the NAR have made their way into many Calvary Chapels — both here in the U.S. and in foreign countries. I have experienced it first-hand on multiple fronts, as many people attending Calvary Chapel have been lured into seeking after supernatural signs and wonders, and other supposed special movements of God. For example, a married couple attending my Bible teaching in 2016 came up one evening after the study to ask my opinion about their recent trip down to LA to attend a large event at a sports venue hosted by two itinerant pastors and the supposedly amazing signs and wonders they did. Upon hearing the names of these two guys, I explained that both were very well-documented false teachers/false prophets, and so I had to ask: "WHY would you ever buy tickets and drive two hours each way to go to their rally?" Our conversation had me focusing in on the sufficiency of God's Word and the truth of God's Holy Spirit dwelling richly in believers all the time, while they kept explaining to me "but the stuff these guys do is just so incredible to see and hear". And I have had similar discussions with dozens of seemingly stable Calvary Chapel attendees who hunted me down by phone, email, or in person to ask my opinion about dozens of NAR personalities featured at healing rallies, let-the-fire-fall services, heaven-come-down miracle crusades, prophetic-word conferences, worship music workshops, and word-of-faith events. My answer remains the same - God's Word will always show the consistency of sound truths, AND will always expose false doctrines.

This book is not designed to be a comprehensive review and analysis of the full history and scope of the overall NAR movement. That has already been done very well by Doug Gievett and Holly Pivec in their 2014 book *A New Apostolic Reformation? A Biblical Response To A Worldwide Movement* (Weaver Books - available at Amazon). They cover ALL of the major topics, doctrines, personalities, churches, and movements with depth, accuracy, Biblical integrity, and well-researched citations. I highly recommend getting your own copy.

Instead, *Entertaining Deception* is specifically focused on discussing the NAR as it relates directly to Calvary Chapel churches. I cover similar topics and themes, but always in the context of the NAR's migration into the specific ministries and mission of Calvary Chapels worldwide. The ten chapters that follow focus on the various dimensions of the NAR's *entertaining deception* and why *entertaining* these false doctrines, practices, movements, and personalities is a direct challenge to the core mission and ministry of Calvary Chapel.

Chapter-1 provides a foundational overview of the Biblical bases for Sound Doctrine, and then Chapter-2 explains how to readily recognize spiritual deception compared to Biblical truth. Chapter-3 introduces the contemporary phenomenon of the NAR, how it got started, its focus on a "new" church age of super prophets and apostles, and how its worldview introduces dangerous deceptions. Chapter-4 provides a Biblical overview of the kinds of signs and wonders the NAR supports, in light of Jesus' searing commentary on any generation that is focused on these. Chapter-5 then lays out a clear distinction between one's personal experiences and the foundational positions of God's Word in readily sorting out deception from truth.

Chapter-6 describes the subtle (and many not so subtle) ways that NAR teachings and practices have already made their way into the various ministries of Calvary Chapel, with a clear Biblical exhortation to church leaders to become pro-active in addressing these and stopping them in their tracks. In Chapter-7, the ministry groups, churches, associations, and networks of the contemporary NAR are named, including the key players, practices, authors, and musicians with their over-emphasis on personal experiences and "elite" Christianity that ALL clearly depart from the core tenets of Biblically sound doctrine. Chapter-8 shows how the NAR directly challenges the core tenets of church life laid out in Pastor Chuck's 2000 book *Calvary Chapel Distinctives* (The Word For Today) and why Calvary Chapels need to be extremely discerning to not allow these to slowly make their way into church life. Chapter-9 provides a strong Biblical basis for the role of Calvary Chapel pastors and elders to be a frontline defense in stepping up as vigilant "over-seers" of the congregation, and to hold fast to sound doctrine and the core distinctives that always defined Calvary Chapel. Chapter-10 concludes by looking at potential ways the NAR could play a major part in the future direction of Calvary Chapel, regarding the issues happening right now between the Calvary Chapel Association (CCA) and the "new" Calvary Chapel Global Network (CCGN). The Appendix has a wide range of Biblically sound resources for deeper research into these topics.

In Matthew 24 Jesus clearly stated that one of the signs leading up to Him coming back for His church would be the rise of MANY false prophets, apostles, and even messiahs whose ability to twist God's Word and spread false teachings would be so crafty and appear so close to the truth that "EVEN THE ELECT WOULD BE DECEIVED". That is a profound warning from our Lord. It would <u>not</u> be a "new" era of spiritually elite super-Christians leading the church into signs and wonders. In his now classic book *Charisma vs. Charismania* (Harvest House, 1983) Pastor Chuck explained the difference between the true work of the Holy Spirit (Biblically sound "charisma" - a "gift" from God), and "charis-*mania*" - trying to do (replicate) the work of the Spirit - calling it *"a spiritual hype that substitutes perspiration for inspiration [using] the genius, energy, and gimmicks of man as a substitute for the wisdom and ability of God".* At the conclusion, he expressed this concerns and caution: *"One of the sad results of charismania is its repelling influence on so many hungry, earnest saints of God. Do not allow the unscriptural excesses of those practicing charismania to discourage you from seeking all that God wants you to experience - the love, joy, and power of living in the fullness of the Spirit ."*

Many people (even at Calvary Chapels) are for some reason yearning for "new" spiritual experiences they believe are needed to get them closer to God. The last chapter of Pastor Chuck's book *Living Water* (The Word for Today, 1996) is titled "The Ultimate Experience", but he wasn't talking about seeking after signs and wonders. Rather, he spoke of simply abiding in Christ, with the example of newly budding apples on a branch that have been cut from the tree.

That fruit never ripens, in fact it dies because it is no longer abiding in (connected to) the source of its life. God's Word is the only source for truth. God cannot contradict His own Word. He gave us the Bible - His personal Word to mankind - so we would have a solid, consistent standard by which to know and understand truth. A place we go to time and again for steady, reliable commentary on everything pertaining to life. When personal experiences line up with - and do not contradict - God's Word, we can then confidently confirm these as genuine and truly a gift from His Spirit. But when someone's "unique" experiences or "new" practices, teachings, ideas, visions, and interpretations do not line up with God's Word, we have the assurance of being able to discern these as not genuine - not in line with sound Biblical truths - and we can judge them to be false. My prayer is that this book will spur you on to be a diligent Berean, searching the Scriptures daily to see if these things are so. And that you would be praying for Calvary Chapel leaders to also be diligent and vigilant defenders of the timeless truths in God's Word.

- David Newton
Santa Barbara, California

CHAPTER ONE
Sound Doctrine

The Basis Of All We Know

Pastor Chuck and the ministry of Calvary Chapel have always been about Biblical truth being crucial to understanding God the Father, Jesus the Son, and the person of the Holy Spirit. Knowing God's Word has always been the basis for Calvary Chapel ministry. The Psalmist declares that the Word of God is upright (33:4) and is treasured in the heart so that we would not sin against the Lord (119:11). God's Word encourages believers to abound in every way in this life (2nd Corinthians 8). Paul strongly encouraged pastor Timothy and fellow missionary Titus to always be sure to "teach sound doctrine" (1st Timothy 4:6, Titus 1:9 and 2:1). The three Greek words for knowledge in the Bible are "gnosis" (γνῶσις), "suneido" (συνείδω), and "akouo" (ἀκούω). Luke used gnosis to describe knowing through observation of facts that lead to firm conclusions. Suneido is about becoming aware of something brought to your attention by others, while akouo simply means to hear and comprehend (the root word of "acoustic"). These are in the Bible over 450 times, so there is obviously a great deal that God wants us to know and understand, and we do.

The Bible says that knowledge will one day [in the future] be done away with (1st Corinthians 13:8), and that by comparison, love is much better than having knowledge alone (1st Corinthians 13:2). When we are finally with the Lord for eternity, there will no longer be a need to interpret the Bible because we will know in full. So even though now we only know in part (2nd Corinthians 2:14) and see through a glass dimly (1st Corinthians 13:12), the Bible does provide all we need at this time. It's complete, not lacking, and presents God's full counsel on everything we need to know. Sound doctrine is clearly laid out in the full context of 66 books written by 40 authors. God's Word is trustworthy in all ways for our instruction, even though God's infinite knowledge is certainly different from - and higher than - that of the world and man's perspectives on God and this life [1st Corinthians 3:19 and Isaiah 55:8-9].

Timeless Truths or Something "New"

This book could have been written 100 years ago and these same topics would also be contemporary to people living in the early 20th century. It would also apply to the 19th century just after the Civil War, the 1700s during the American Revolution, the 1400s Renaissance in Europe, and according to Rabbi Paul (Saul) of Tarsus, it was spot on for both Jewish and Gentile churches in the middle of the 1st Century A.D. That's because there have always been false teachers and practices of man competing for the attention of Christians. If the first church in Judea under the leadership of Peter and James - or the newer church-plants in Ephesus, Corinth, and Rome under the guidance of Paul — had been perfect in everything they said and did, with no challenges to the sound doctrine upon which they were founded, we might today feel as though the early Christians could not have imagined all the crazy, troubling, awkward stuff going on in the church today. But teaching and holding onto sound doctrine is one of the most popular topics covered for the churches in the New Testament. As we search the Scriptures for pastoral perspectives on how to deal with falsehood, it is actually encouraging to realize that none of the false teachings happening today in the church is actually "new" - in fact they are actually just more and more of the same old lies, prideful boasts, and twisting of God's Word that have been around since the birth of the church. The Apostle Paul notes this eleven specific times to young pastor Timothy in Ephesus, and Paul's missionary companion Titus. He also warned the Ephesian church to *"not be tossed here and there by every wind of [false] doctrine"* - noting such comes from the *"trickery of man, through craftiness, and deceitful scheming".*

Sound doctrine was needed 2,000 years ago and it's certainly still needed today, and must have a prominent role in the daily life of Christians everywhere. Psalm 40 reminds us God's Word is the rock upon which we stand to have sure footing. Hebrews 4 notes that God's Word is living, active, and sharp enough to divide truth from falsehood. Paul's second letter to Timothy defines God's Word as sufficient for [sound] doctrine, reproof and correction [of false doctrine], and timeless instruction in righteousness. It provides the very basis for vibrant church life. Sound doctrine solidifies how we know and understand God's Word with consistency. It establishes the footing for active ministry in the world, maintaining a solid consistency for how pastors, elders, and lay leaders teach the Bible. It's sad when sound doctrine gets relegated to a lesser position, a lower priority, or a fringe topic - typically under the rationale that as Christians we should "emphasize what unites us, not what divides us". Don't get me wrong, I'm all for working together and partnering in outreach ministries with other churches. But that has to be very carefully established, nurtured, and maintained along common principles of sound doctrine that align our hearts and minds with God's Word. And even more importantly, we must cultivate sound doctrine within our own church to ensure that consistency in every form of ministry, with no mixed messages happening among people regarding core Biblical truths that have stood the tests of time.

Teach The Same

Pastor Chuck had the same commitment as Paul - that the Gospel had to be taught with great care to ensure the consistency of sound doctrine throughout all areas of Calvary Chapel. *"The things which you have heard from*

22

me in the presence of many witnesses, entrust these to faithful men who will be able to teach others also" (2nd Timothy 2:2). When Pastor Chuck, like Paul, encourages church leaders to "teach that which was taught to you" it's because the Bible uses the term "didasko" (διδάσκω in the Greek), which inherently means "teach the SAME thing". It's understood that the heart of "teaching" someone is always about passing along the exact same knowledge received from the one who taught you. Greek scholars note it's inferred that this is homo-didasko ("homo" = same). That's why false doctrine is captured using the wording "hetero-didasko" (ἕτερο in the Greek) meaning to teach something "different" than what was taught to you. Paul reminded young Pastor Timothy, *"In pointing out these things to the brethren, you will be a good servant of Christ Jesus, constantly nourished on the words of the faith and of the sound doctrine which you have been following"* (1st Timothy 4:6). Paul said the same thing to Titus, *"hold fast the faithful word which is in accordance with the teaching, being able both to exhort in sound doctrine and to refute those who contradict"* (Titus 1:9). When the church hears God's Word in that consistent manner, this is sound doctrine. It's reliable and people can count on it not deviating from core truths and foundational principles.

Calvary Chapel has always been a place where "homo"-didasko took place, as Pastor Chuck discipled others, teaching them timeless Biblical truths, and they went on to disciple and teach others, who did the same, and so on as that verse-by-verse expository teaching through the entire Bible (Genesis to Revelation, and then start again) became a hallmark of Calvary Chapel. The nine men noted in Pastor Chuck's 2005 book *Harvest* (co-author Tal Brooke) highlighted this wonderfully Biblical discipleship process Chuck had with Greg Laurie, Steve Mays, Jon Courson, Raul Ries, Jeff Johnson, Skip Heitzig, Bil Gallatin, Joe Focht, and Mike MacIntosh. The growth of Calvary Chapel was not about Pastor Chuck imparting some "new" experiences he came up with, rather it was him teaching sound doctrine from God's Word that radically changed the lives of these young men, who then matured in their walk with Jesus, and were raised up to disciple and teach a next generation, and this repeated (multiplied) as God continued to call men out from that Biblical mentoring into pastoring their own churches where they equipped men and women to do the ministry.

My 33 years in Calvary Chapel are summarized at the end of this book. The common theme throughout every ministry area in which I was involved was always "growing and maturing in the knowledge of God's Word". Different teachers, each teaching through different books of the Bible, each with their own unique teaching style, slides, handouts, workbooks, or study notes. And yet there was always an amazing consistency that was readily cross-referenced and confirmed, because the sound doctrine validated time and again the clear message of God's Word [the Logos] - from Genesis to Revelation.

Sound doctrine does not contradict itself, and it never suddenly allows something "new" to be introduced that is "hetero" or not aligned with the time-tested principles and practical applications. As I grew in wisdom and knowledge of God's Word, opportunities opened for me to begin teaching others the same sound Biblical truths that I had been taught ("homo"-didasko). In each of these different venues I had my own teaching style, developed my own slides, and brought my university B-school professor approach into how I prepared, while using the Socratic Method to stir up interest among those attending my Bible studies. But at the core of my teaching was always sound doctrine, timeless truths, and consistency with the principles I had been taught and discipled in.

The LOGOS

The Bible presents God's very own Word to mankind as a rock, a firm foundation upon which we build, even as the loose sands of the world's teachings have no solid footing and are constantly shifting (Matthew 7:24-27), even as the waves around us are tossed about to and fro (James 1:6), and the winds have strong gusts that move things out of place (Ephesians 4:14). False doctrine is random, unpredictable, unstable - even as Jesus recognized the unseen evil forces that were behind the wind and huge waves on the Sea of

Galilee when He "rebuked" that storm (Mark 4:39). False doctrine (hetero-didasko, different teaching) is the "every wind of doctrine" that blows in and blows out again, the unstable sand under one's feet, the waves that toss all about. Contrary to those Biblical images, God's Word is a lamp shining on our steps, it lights the path on which we walk (Psalm 119:105). God cannot lie, so His Word is trustworthy and reliable (Psalm 33:4) - because Jesus is the same yesterday, today, and forever (Hebrews 13:8). What He says is an anchor to our soul (Hebrews 6:17-18) that holds firm against all those forces that would try to constantly move us from one position to another.

Teaching timeless truths from God's Word has always been the core ministry of Calvary Chapel. The Greek root word for "doctrine" is "didache" (διδαχή). It literally means "instruction". The Holy Spirit does didache for those in whom He dwells (1st John 2:27). The early church devoted themselves to the Apostles' didache (Acts 2:42). Christians should be ready in season and out to reprove, rebuke, and exhort based upon didache (2nd Timothy 4:2) that is sound in its content (Titus 1:9). Pastor Chuck loved to say that "healthy sheep will reproduce" - based on Jesus' exhortation to Peter in John 21 to "feed my sheep" ("tend my lambs"). Sound doctrine is a common denominator that unifies the church, so that everyone from the senior pastor and assistant pastors, to the youth pastors, elders, and deacons, as well as the Sunday school teachers, home Bible study leaders, and any others involved in ministry and leadership will deliver a consistent message from God's Word.

Perhaps sound doctrine can be summed up in Pastor Chuck's 1989 paper *Philosophy Of Ministry*, where he explains that in Ephesians 4 he found how "God placed gifted men, for the perfecting of the saints for the work of the ministry, the building up of the body of Christ. This brought in a philosophical change as far as my concept of the purpose of the church. Rather than seeing the primary purpose as evangelization, I saw that the purpose of the church was for the perfecting of the saints, making the believers strong, bringing them into maturity, feeding them, loving them, strengthening them so that they would be engaged in the work of the ministry. In changing my philosophy, I began to teach the Word of God in a consistent way designed to produce growth within the believers. When the saints were perfected for the work of the ministry, they began to minister, to bring in friends, and evangelism became the by-product of a strong and mature church. It's the natural function of healthy sheep to reproduce. When you make the sheep healthy by giving them a good diet [of God's Word], a consistent diet that will develop growth and strength, they will naturally reproduce". The next chapter examines spiritual deception - those false teachings that are the exact opposite of sound doctrine, and how subtle changes introduced by men will lead the sheep away from Biblical truth.

CHAPTER TWO
Spiritual Deception

The Root Of All Deception

The previous chapter focused on the need to teach sound doctrine — to ensure that those things that were taught to us will in fact be preserved in content and taught to others. But Paul understood there would be problems in the church *"for the time will come when they will not endure sound doctrine, but wanting to have their ears tickled, they will accumulate for themselves teachers in accordance to their own desires"* [2nd Timothy 4:3]. He recognized that men would have a tendency to move away from sound doctrine, such that *"if anyone advocates a different doctrine and does not agree with sound words, those of our Lord Jesus Christ, and with the doctrine conforming to godliness, he is conceited and understands nothing, but [instead] he has a morbid interest in controversial questions and disputes about words, out of which arise envy, strife, abusive language, evil suspicions, and constant friction between men of depraved mind, deprived of the truth, who suppose that godliness is a means of gain"* (1st Timothy 6:3-5). This is exactly what we see when false teaching and spiritual deception are introduced within the church.

Paul also warned the church leaders in Colossae, *"See to it that no one takes you captive through philosophy and empty deception, according to the tradition of men, according to the elementary principles of the world, rather than according to Christ"* [Colossians 2:8]. Spiritual deception is at the root of false doctrine. Deception means "to represent something that is counterfeit as if it were true". The church has been warned that Satan uses the deception of wickedness with power, signs, and wonders (2nd Thessalonians 2:9-10). It is a sure reminder that Satan will use his power and craftiness to undermine the Word of God. As with these, hindrances and dissensions find their way into the church through *entertaining deception* (Romans 16:17-18). John stated clearly the reason he wrote the truths about God was because there were those trying *intentionally* to deceive [1st John 2:26] - this is Satan's work (1st John 3:7-8). In fact, the very reason Satan is removed from the world at Christ's second coming to rule in Jerusalem is to ensure *"he will no longer be able to deceive the nations"* (Revelation 20:3). His deception remains the same today - that he exchanges the truth of God for a lie (Romans 1:25).

This is the primary purpose of Lucifer's efforts against those who believe in Jesus. Obvious lies can be quickly recognized by Christians as false. But the devil also works in subtle ways that may not be obvious to those who lack in spiritual discernment. This is his way of introducing falsehood into the church. Paul reminds us that Satan is able to disguise and present himself as an "angel of light" (2nd Corinthians 11:14). His craft is the ability to carefully repackage falsehood in such a way that it has the appearance of truth. The more subtle the turning away from Biblical truth, the more difficult it is to recognize. God clearly wants Christians to be readily able to discern false teachings from sound doctrine. His Word is the only basis by which lies can be spiritually discerned. Why? Because the Word of God is living and active and sharper than any two-edged sword, piercing as far as the division of the spirit and the soul, and able to judge the thoughts and intentions of the heart (Hebrews 4:12). The solid food of the Bible is for those who are spiritually mature, because they spend regular time in the Word and have their senses trained to discern good from evil (Hebrews 5:14). Believers should abound in knowledge and all discernment, to approve what is excellent, and be sincere and blameless until the day of Christ (Philippians 1:9-10). One of the gifts of the Holy Spirit is distinguishing (discerning) spirits (1st Corinthians 12:10). John admonished believers to *"not believe every spirit, but test the spirits to see whether they are from God, because many false prophets have gone out into the world"* (1st John 4:1). We must be supernaturally empowered to distinguish truth from a lie. The basis of sound church life is sound doctrine that speaks to every aspect of ministry, service, worship, administration, and leadership.

Same As The First Century

Jesus stated very clearly [in quoting Isaiah] that *"you honor me with your lips, but your heart is far from me, for in vain you worship me, teaching as doctrine the mere precepts of men"* (Matthew 15:8-9). In the same way Paul encouraged Timothy about *"teaching what I taught you"*, he also clearly urged all pastors and church leaders to *"instruct certain men not to teach strange doctrines, nor to pay attention to myths and endless genealogies which give rise to mere speculation [because] the goal of our instruction is love from a pure heart and a good conscience and a sincere faith"*. He then pens this to REALLY get our attention: *"but some men, straying from this, have turned aside to fruitless discussion, wanting to be teachers, even though they do not understand either what they are saying or the matters about which they make confident assertions"* (1st Timothy 3:1-7). Yes, even in the 1st Century church there were those who first, strayed from sound doctrine (those foundational things they had been taught); second, they turned aside to fruitless discussion [about things other than the Word of God], and third, while they wanted to be teachers themselves, Paul clarifies that they did not even understand the things they said [the statements they made - doctrines they introduced], or the matters about which they made such confident assertions. They strayed from sound doctrine and moved instead into the fruitless discussions of man, while trying to teach others about things they didn't even understand. The Spirit says [1st Timothy 4] *"in succeeding seasons there will be MANY DEPARTING from the faith paying attention to deceitful spirits and doctrine of demons, by means of the hypocrisy of liars seared in their own conscience as with a branding iron. In pointing out these things to the brethren, you will be a good servant of Christ Jesus, constantly nourished on words of faith and the sound doctrine which you have been following. Prescribe and teach these things . . . In speech, conduct, love, faith, purity – be an example of those who believe".*

Twenty centuries later, that very same temptation to wander away from sound doctrine is still happening. In fact Jesus notes that in the time just prior to His coming for the church, *"false messiahs and false prophets will arise, and will show great signs and wonders, so as to mislead if possible even the elect"* (Matthew 24:24). The logical response to Jesus is "How could that happen?" Well, Bill Johnson from Bethel Church openly encourages people to set aside sound knowledge [doctrine] while allowing that "our hearts can embrace things that our heads can't [so] our hearts will lead us where *our logic would never dare to go,* because to follow [the Holy Spirit], we must be willing to follow OFF THE MAP, to go beyond what we know" (Christian Research Journal, Vol. 37-No. 5, 2014). His position is entirely false and epitomizes *entertaining deception.* We HAVE that clear map - the Bible - and God's Holy Spirit will never contradict

God's own Word, so we will never be led "off that map" by the Holy Spirit. You never have to embrace deception that your head knows is untrue, while instead following after your heart [emotions]. There's no need to go beyond the sound doctrine you know - as if there's something more - into areas where you don't know, because God's Word IS that map that guides and keeps us in truth.

The Spiritual Core of Mankind

People are significantly unique in God's creation because of the words, "Let Us Make Man In Our Image" [Genesis 1:26]. So while the living creations in the animal kingdom have a physical body and brain consciousness (two dimensions), Paul notes the unique three-dimensional nature of mankind made in God's image [1st Thessalonians 5:23] with a body ("soma" in the Greek), our consciousness (the "psuche" - root word for *psychology*), and our spirit (the "pneuma"). The Bible is God's Word, defined as the "pneuma" (breath) of God [2nd Timothy 3:16 literally says *theo-pneuma* in the Greek, or "God-breathed"]. The Holy Spirit is the "Pneuma", and when Adam was formed, God breathed (*theo-pneuma*) into his nostrils and he became a living being. In John 20:22 Jesus breathed (*Pneuma*) on his disciples and said "Receive the Holy Spirit". John opens his gospel by describing Jesus as the "Word" — the *Logos* (λόγος) in Greek. And the Bible is also the *Logos* - the Word of God. That's why the Bible can make such an amazing connection when we read it, because there is a unique spiritual dimension as God's Word speaks directly to our spirit, clearly communicating timeless truths for encouragement, instruction, reproof, correction, admonition. That's also why we can have fellowship (κοινωνία = koinonia in Greek) with one another through the Holy Spirit when we assemble together to study God's Word. When it is taught properly, with great care to hold fast to sound doctrine, it is confirmed as right and good in our spirit, by the Holy Spirit. But when it STRAYS from sound doctrine or TURNS ASIDE to fruitless discussion, the spiritually discerning individual will immediately recognize that this is not right, while the undiscerning person is easily led away *"tossed here and there by waves, carried about by **every wind of doctrine, by the trickery of** men, by craftiness in deceitful scheming"* [Ephesians 4:14].

Our Sinful Nature

The definition of sin is simply "to miss the mark". The imagery is of one who aims at the target pulling back on the bowstring, and then releases the arrow, but it doesn't even make it to the target. It completely misses the mark. It falls short. The original sin in God's created order occurred when the beautiful "anointed cherub that covers" - Lucifer - reasoned that he could aspire to and attain the same exalted position of God. Isaiah, writing prophetically about this "shining one", the "star of the morning", "son of the dawn" (in Hebrew, the *Heylel*), explains that he coveted the position of God as something for himself (Isaiah 14) - essentially reasoning that he could be just like God. For that disobedience to God's Word, he was cast down from heaven to the earth, along with one-third of the heavenly hosts who also followed his disobedience. This very being, in his fallen state, came to Eve in Eden and made the exact same presentation – that God's Word was not exactly what she understood it to be, and that she too could be just like God. Lucifer repeats this offer once more directly to Jesus when he encounters our Lord fasting in the wilderness, appealing to the Messiah to not be obedient to God the Father, while twisting the Word of God in outright spiritual deception.

That Same "Old" Offer

Throughout the Bible, in every occurrence of spiritual deception, false doctrine, errant teaching, inaccurate prophetic words, misleading interpretation of Scripture, and presenting lies as truth, there are those whose hearts and minds are open to such (described as spiritually undiscerning), and those who immediately recognize that the teaching, preaching, or prophecy does not line up with the timeless truths of God's own Word (they have spiritual discernment). 1st John 2:16 helps to clarify that the original sin of Lucifer's disobedience, the disobedience of Eve and then Adam, Satan's attempt to persuade Jesus to disobey, and our own inherent sinful nature as being these same three things: 1) the lust of the flesh, 2) the lust of the eyes, and 3) the boastful pride of life.

Satan's offer to Jesus was: 1) satisfy your flesh and turn the stones into bread; 2) see God's protection by dropping from the top of the Temple in Jerusalem so angels will protect you; and 3) to boast as the earthly king ruling over all the nations of the world, if Jesus would simply bow down and worship. That common thread remains in place today. People want the attention, the adoration, the glory attributed to them. They desire to be exalted above others. Spiritual deception comes from those who wander off the map of God's Word, and teach the precepts of man as if they were doctrine [Matthew 15:9].

Plumb-Line and Level

One of the best features of God's Word is that it time and again serves as both a plumb-line AND a level. We can lay any kind of teaching, movement, worship, or signs alongside God's Word to see clearly whether or not these align with sound doctrine. Whenever we observe some kind of "new" religious topic, and God's Holy Spirit witnesses to our hearts and minds that this doesn't seem to be straight up, we can apply God's Word - sound doctrine - alongside the book, sermon, song lyrics, or prophecy and the Bible remains the top-to-bottom plumb line that defines the perfect positioning, with no leaning to one side or the other. And it is just like a perfectly calibrated level that when laid on any object will immediately either confirm the soundness of the surface, or show it leaning to some degree of incline away from "true" level. Building contractors, design engineers, architects - even typical homeowners doing a project around the house — all have times when the temptation is to simply "eye-ball" the edge of a wall, a window, or doorway to see if it's straight up and down. But nothing is better than having that indisputable plumb line held right alongside the edge as the fixed standard that defines if something is straight or not. How many of us have "approximated" the hanging of a picture frame, mirror, towel rack, or shelf that *seemed* level, only to lay the true level on that surface to find we were off a few degrees to one side?

The lesson is clearly noted: without a reliable gauge against which to compare something, we're left to our personal perceptions to decide whether something is straight up or level — and there will always be some margin of error with our own perceptions. But if we systematically use that reliable marker for what's "true" we will consistently be correct in our review of any doctrine or experience. Luke noted that the Bible is in fact the "full counsel" of God, with tremendous consistency of the Old Testament revealed in the New Testament, even as Messiah and the Church were concealed in Israel's Torah, the Psalms, and the Prophets. Pastor Chuck always said, "the very best commentary on the Bible is . . . the Bible". Such a simple axiom, and yet false teachings are almost always generated and built upon one stand-alone passage completely out of context from the "full counsel" of the Word. One action by someone once in a single Bible verse is often used as THE foundational basis for a whole "new" way to pray, to worship, to receive the Holy Spirit, to heal someone, or to see and hear God. Virtually all the DVDs, podcasts, CDs, and other teaching media available online from false teachers has very little to do with a deep, exegetical review and exposition of God's Word. Instead there is one verse, or even just a portion of a single verse, used as a jumping off point to say just about anything they want, OR there's no Scripture at all, as the "teacher" simply recounts personal experiences of going up to heaven, hearing God's voice in the middle of the night, regularly speaking with angels, and similar signs and wonders.

The Doctrinal Continuum

Spiritual deception can be easily mapped. Figure 2.1 illustrates the positioning of sound doctrine and false teachings. Biblical truth that has stood the test of time is located on the far right. On the opposite end over to the left

Figure 2.1

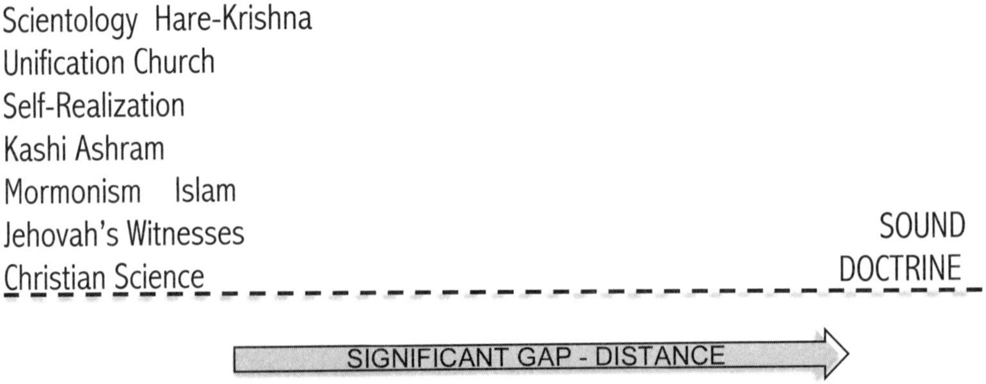

Scientology Hare-Krishna
Unification Church
Self-Realization
Kashi Ashram
Mormonism   Islam
Jehovah's Witnesses
Christian Science

SOUND
DOCTRINE

SIGNIFICANT GAP - DISTANCE ⟹

are various cults, psychics, pseudo-churches, and other movements that are deceptively and incorrectly trying to be linked to the Bible, or have their own form of "sacred", "inspired" writings. Dozens more could be added as they loosely hold to one or more topics from the Bible (for example, many false religions believe: Jesus was crucified, or that God is the Creator of the universe, or a covenant was made with Abraham). But generally, such false teachings are readily, easily recognized due to the preponderance of unsupported (out of context) principles and/or fanciful claims made by the founder. As such, there have been hundreds of books written on these cults and aberrant movements, all clearly exposing them as false teachings with no Biblical basis. They are the polar opposites of sound doctrine, typically very far-removed from God's Word.

However, a very "slippery slope" is exposed in Figure 2.2, where certain types of false teachings and spiritual deception are designed to cozy up right

Figure 2.2

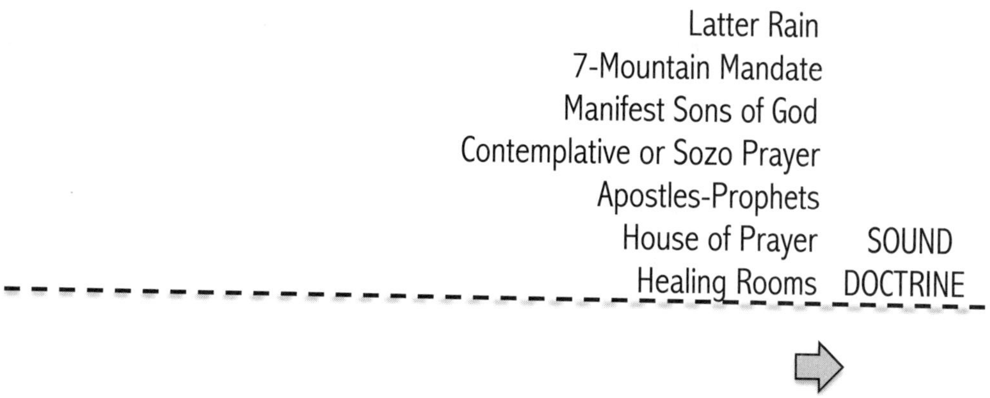

Latter Rain
7-Mountain Mandate
Manifest Sons of God
Contemplative or Sozo Prayer
Apostles-Prophets
House of Prayer   SOUND
Healing Rooms   DOCTRINE

next to sound doctrine. This close proximity has the outward [but false] façade that appears very similar to sound doctrine, using similar terminology such as "holiness", "the Presence", "glory", "heaven come down", "the kingdom of God", "a house devoted to 24/7 prayer", "healing", "visions", "dreams" and "developing greater faith". On their thin surfaces, these concepts (doctrines) seem to have all the right buzzwords, a scriptural quote, (albeit entirely out of context), and plenty of enthusiasm and apparent sincerity. But the reality is that coming up close is not the same as BEING sound truth. If some church movement, prophet, apostle, or pastor is off a lot, but another is only off a little, they are still both OFF. In fact, the more subtle the spiritual deception (due to closer proximity to sound doctrine), the more difficult it will be to identify it as false teaching. The most disconcerting problem of so many contemporary deceptions is how they appear "okay" to the average person.

The next chapter introduces the modern movement known as the New Apostolic Reformation (referred to as NAR throughout this book). This will review the basics concepts regarding the underlying philosophy and Biblical worldview that drives this movement, while Chapter Six provides more details about specific NAR doctrines and practices. Chapter Seven will then cover the who's who among today's NAR churches and personalities.

CHAPTER THREE
The New Apostolic Reformation

Something "New" (Again)

The last twenty centuries are littered with the notoriety of men and women who represented themselves to the church and the world as having received some "new" revelation from God, to which hundreds, thousands, even millions of people then flocked, searching for an opportunity to be part of the next special generation of Christians who are more spiritual, closer to God, and able to effect supernatural signs and wonders on earth in the same manner of the First Century Apostles. The latest version of this phenomenon is the New Apostolic Reformation (NAR) - which is not really "new" at all, but just more of the same old false doctrines and pastors-teachers-prophets-apostles of the last two millennia, going all the way back to the same cast of characters Paul and Peter encountered alongside the early church. The NAR has been described by those leading this movement as the "Third Wave", referring to its place in time after the First Wave (classic Pentecostalism, often linked to the 1906 Azusa Street revivals in Los Angeles), and the Second Wave (the 1960s charismatic movement of signs and wonders that occurred in mainline denominational churches). The Third Wave is defined as starting in the 1980s with a "new" signs and wonders era promoted by two key personalities: John Wimber and C. Peter Wagner. Wimber's initial church, Vineyard Christian Fellowship in Anaheim, was a part of Calvary Chapel, but he soon parted ways with Pastor Chuck who did not agree with the "charismania" John wanted to pursue and his "kingdom now" theology. Wimber then joined Kenn Gulliksen's Vineyard movement [Gulliksen's 1974 Vineyard Fellowship in West Los Angeles was also originally a Calvary Chapel church-plant]. On the other hand, Wagner was a professor at Fuller Seminary where he co-founded a new course (with Wimber) titled: *Signs, Wonders, And Church Growth.* Wagner then defined his books and lectures as "the New Apostolic Reformation" and that label stuck. The NAR is closely linked to the "the Emerging Church" [also "Emergent"] - a broad description for the churches that conform their message to fit the cultural changes happening in society, catering to a younger generation that is looking for more relevancy and tangible identity in how they contribute to - and are part of - God's kingdom.

The NAR is profoundly egocentric when you consider the three words Wagner used to define his movement. First, it's "New". False doctrines and their teachers always say they are "new", something that's never been done before, a special work of God that has never happened previously, with unique insights that no one else has ever had about God and spiritual life. Second, it's

"Apostolic". Short of being the next Messiah, they have anointed themselves as Apostles with the same spiritual authority as the 1st Century Apostles. And third, it's a "Reformation" - a clear reference that Wagner desires to be known in history right alongside Martin Luther, who in the 16th Century initiated the Protestant split from the Roman Catholic Church. As such, Wagner has positioned himself as that anointed agent of spiritual change directly charged by God to "reform" the church through a brand "new" ministry built on his self-declared "Apostolic" authority. He elevated himself to the title "presiding Apostle" to exercise personal interpretations for spiritual direction for the church worldwide. Many quickly followed his lead and joined Wagner as "new" Apostles also, while fantastic-miraculous signs and wonders became the criteria for membership into this elite fraternity of specially equipped Christians. They claim to travel regularly in the spirit to heaven to commune with Jesus, angelic beings, and various Biblical personalities who share all kinds of "new" revelations and prophecies that go far beyond what's already in God's Word.

Bookends Of The Church Age

The NAR Apostles truly believe that the original 12 Apostles are the First Century bookend supporting the beginning of the New Testament Church, while they now comprise the 21st Century bookend supporting the other end that will wrap up the Church Age. They place themselves in the same spiritual position as Peter, John, and Paul. In their 1988 recordings titled *Visions And Revelations,* NAR apostle Mike Bickle recounts a visit to heaven by "Kansas City Prophet" Bob Jones with this: "The Apostle Paul was anxious to talk to the end-times apostles and prophets because what they [the NAR apostles] would do would do *far more* to the glory of God, and the saints in the New Testament would wait in line to greet the apostles from this [current] generation". Could a statement be any more egocentric, conceited, prideful, and boasting then to claim the Apostles Paul, Peter, John, Philip, Thomas, and others are awestruck and admiring of these NAR apostles and prophets, and will be standing in line up in heaven to greet the NAR elite? Perhaps rather than waiting for the Apostles Paul and Peter to shake hands and greet them, NAR leaders should read the Bible's explicit warnings about false teachers and spiritual deception: *"If we or an angel from heaven should preach to you a gospel contrary to the one we preached to you, let him be accursed"* (Galatians 1:8); *"False prophets arose among the people, just as there will be false teachers among you, who will secretly bring in destructive heresies, even denying the Master who bought them, bringing upon themselves swift destruction; many will follow their sensuality - because of them the way of truth will be blasphemed. In their greed they will exploit you with false words. Their condemnation from long ago is not idle, and their destruction is not asleep"* (2nd Peter 2:1-3).

Sound doctrine is readily found throughout the Bible, and anything else originating from another source is by definition deception, for even "Satan can disguise himself as an angel of light" (2nd Corinthians 11:14). The NAR has now brought its "Third Wave" emphasis on apostles, prophets, signs and wonders, and special revelations right to the front door (and inside) of Calvary Chapel.

Wagner Defines The NAR

Before his death in October 2016, C. Peter Wagner wrote dozens of books describing how God chose him as the catalyst for this "new" movement of modern apostles, prophets, miracles, signs, and wonders. In his 1998 book *Apostles Today: Biblical Government For Biblical Power* he wrote: "We are now living in the midst of one of the most epochal changes in the structure of the Church that has ever been recorded - I call it 'The Second Apostolic Age'". The promotional introduction for his 1999 book *Church Quake! The Explosive Power Of The New Apostolic Reformation* beckons: "A revolution is taking place, an extraordinary work of God that is changing the shape of Christianity around the world - the New Apostolic Reformation is a grassroots phenomenon in which God is raising up alliances of non-denominational churches and leaders to help fulfill the last awesome push for the Great Commission, [where] present-day Apostolic church networks are bound together not by doctrine or tradition, but by shared passion for local and worldwide evangelism, energetic worship, fervent prayer, and church planting" (notice the key words *not by doctrine*).

Once Wagner positioned himself as a "new" Apostle, the door was wide open for many others to enter into that same self-defined position, drawn by the elevated status that comes in joining Wagner as an elite class of Christians who have special spiritual gifting. Today these super-Apostles are listed at the Global Apostolic Registry (GAR) - also the Global Apostolic Network (GAN) that assures members *"our ministry credentials and certificates are recognized and respected in all fifty states in the USA and in most every major country of the world"*. There's the Wagner Leadership Institute - *"an international network of apostolic training centers established to equip the saints for kingdom ministry"*. The Global Apostolic Impact Network (GAIN) [also Latter Rain Assembly] places people in one of three successive levels: Membership, Maturity, or Ministry, and offers courses in its Apostolic Training School (ATS). The International Coalition of Apostolic Leaders (ICAL) says *"applicants must be nominated by two current members and fit the description of an Apostle stated above. After completing the appropriate applications, an ICAL official will interview the nominee and review the application on a national, continental, or international basis - depending upon the applicant's geography and ICAL's presence in their locale"*. This well-crafted NAR pyramid scheme began with Wagner and his close-in circle self-ordaining each other, then like all multi-level marketing networks, once you get just a few layers out from the original individuals at the hub, the domino effect kicks in and the Apostles began to multiply exponentially.

Elijah List

Most, if not all, of the Apostles and Prophets ordained, sanctioned, recognized, and granted memberships by the previous organizations do their apostolic declarations and prophetic forecasts online at ElijahList.com — which includes website banner ads such as: "FREE - Do YOU want more Prophetic words LIKE THIS ONE sent daily to your email inbox?" or "1,000+ WEEKLY delivered from this spirit" and of course "Wearable Prophetic Worship Art". They post daily prophecies about all kinds of incredible-sensational predictions and words from God (that's funny, I thought the Bible, the Logos, was the complete Word of God - so what else is there?). What's really troubling is how the NAR Apostles and Prophets track their own success rates, in the same way major league baseball lists the top hitters in both the National and American leagues. The "top" and "most experienced" apostles boast that their prophetic accuracy is in the range of 65 percent — two out of every three are supposedly correct. Kansas City Prophet Bob Jones has said a prophet only needs to be correct about 60 percent of the time, and that some prophets will in fact "shoot blanks" as they develop their gifting. Perhaps they should consult the Bible about prophets who are anything less than 100 percent correct [Luke 6:26; Ezekiel 13:9; Jeremiah 23:16; 1st John 4:1; Deuteronomy 13:1-5; 18:20-22]. The website states *"If You're Not In Open Rebellion Against God, What He Prophesies Over You Will Come True ... Eventually".* These are such convenient ways out for an unfulfilled (pending) prophecy by member Apostles, because if a wild predictive-word doesn't come true, they weren't wrong, it was the person in "open rebellion against God" that caused the completion-fulfillment to not happen. And if they don't come to pass right away, "Eventually" provides that buffer of weeks, months, even years for fulfillment to occur. The NAR Apostles and Prophets also define any challenge to their authority as "the Jezebel Spirit" (based on the wife of King Ahab who persecuted God's prophets), so that anyone (like me, this book) that *"comes against the true prophetic flow of God hates the prophets and their prophetic ministries".* Again, this is convenient to position themselves with either: "you support and endorse my prophecies", or "you must then have 'The Jezebel Spirit' working in you".

Replacement Theology

The NAR holds firmly to the position that the still unfulfilled promises to Israel found in the Bible are not literal for a future time after the rapture, during a period of judgment on the earth, or when Jesus reigns from David's throne in Jerusalem for ten centuries. Instead they are allegorical, and being fulfilled by

Christians in the current church age. This opens up all kinds of doors that allow the NAR to reinterpret Bible prophecy as ALL about them and their followers. Replacement theology then has direct ramifications in the following NAR beliefs.

Kingdom Now Dominionism

The NAR uses classic replacement theology to say the contemporary church must reclaim the fallen earth and establish a "Christian" world so that Jesus can come back again because His bride (the church) has finally attained perfection and made herself pure and ready for Him. This is also referred to as *Reconstructionism*, as the one true NAR church has been tasked by God with re-building the sinful world into a glorious Christian world with believers occupying every facet of society, redeeming those for God's "Kingdom-Now". Once the church gets that taken care of, Jesus can finally stop waiting up in heaven and return again to the earth for His second coming.

Latter Rain

The NAR embraces the teachings of William Branham, who in the 1930s through 1950s claimed that he was the prophet Elijah returned to earth, and while the Holy Spirit's work in Jerusalem from Acts chapter 2 was the "Early Rain", he was now overseeing a "Second Pentecost" as the Holy Spirit poured down a "Latter Rain" in preparing the church to take kingdom-now dominion of the earth. He based his ministry on taking Joel 2:28 out of the 'Israel' context, using instead a replacement theology viewpoint that ascribes this to the church: *"And it shall come to pass afterward, that I will pour out my spirit upon all flesh; and your sons and your daughters shall prophesy, your old men shall dream dreams, your young men shall see visions".* This is similar to how the Jehovah's Witnesses use replacement theology to stake their belief that the 144,000 in Revelation 7:4-10 are not the literal, clearly noted 12,000 Jewish believers from each of Israel's twelve tribes, but are instead their "special" movement.

Manifest Sons Of God

The NAR then teaches that the church must become progressively more and more purified through signs, wonders, dreams, visions, and miracles — through magnificent displays of praise and worship in the Tabernacle of David that draws down from heaven "the Presence" of God among men. As the church becomes mature, perfected, and sinless it will raise up a "new" (there's that word again) class of elite youth who are the "elect seed" possessing supernatural spiritual abilities (Joel 2:28 sons and daughters prophesying and seeing visions). They will have a global impact, and be the prime catalyst for Jesus returning to earth. These youth [sons and daughters] are the "Manifest Sons Of God" who emerge as the Biblical "overcomers" who will step right into immortality while bringing the Kingdom of God to earth. The NAR's replacement theology also sees this "new" *generation rising up to take its place* (a popular worship song heralds them) as fulfillment of the "man-child" from Revelation 12 (also called the "many-membered man-child"), where becoming a "son of God" has nothing to do with the New Testament's sound doctrine of believers being adopted into the family of God through Christ's finished work on the cross, but is instead all about higher spiritual revelations and stages of maturity that ultimately result in people attaining that position as a "son".

Joel's Army

The NAR then anoints this youth movement (elite sons and daughters) of super worshippers and miracle workers as Joel's Army (from the same Joel 2 passage). NAR Apostle Rick Joyner's 1989 book *The Harvest: Strategic Vision For Mobilizing The Army Of God* uses replacement theology to reinterpret Joel's prophecy about Israel as being about the young people of today being raised up as God's army. NAR Apostles and prophets agree that these will be immortal and will become "like God", as the army literally becomes Christ to the world.

Bridal Eschatology

The NAR's positions on "end times Bible prophecy" is then summed up as a *Bridal eschatology* that focuses entirely on the work efforts of the church (the bride) to get herself purified and ready for the bridegroom. In fact, dozens of NAR books, CDs, podcasts, sermons, and articles all describe Jesus as up in heaven, somewhat frustrated that the church is still not yet ready for Him to be released to come down to earth. All the responsibility for the Lord's 2nd Coming now rests with the NAR leadership to hasten the day by raising up the "new" true church to make ready the way of the Lord. This again involves their egocentric self-exaltation that "as John the Baptist was that voice crying in the wilderness, 'prepare the way of the Lord', so too we [NAR apostles] are a voice in this latter time also crying out 'prepare the way of the Lord'" (from the NAR's Mike Bickle *Prepare The Way Today*, which also includes his teaching on the NAR's "Exodus Cry" and modern day Cities of Refuge – ALL co-opting Israel's promises from the Lord as replacement theology promises to their church).

Seven Mountain Mandate

In the 1970s, *Campus Crusade for Christ* founder Bill Bright introduced his vision for Christian young people coming from college-university studies to go into the world and take up key leadership positions all across the workplace to influence secular society in a positive way for Jesus. His "7 Mountains That Influence Culture" were business, education, government, religion, family, arts and entertainment, and the media. I was at that time a student at The King's College in Briarcliff Manor, NY (during the tenure of President Robert Cook), and that exhortation became part of a King's education, as faculty encouraged us, regardless of undergraduate major, to let the Lord lead-guide-direct into strategic institutions where we would be lights in a dark place, and like salt to the world. The NAR has co-opted (commandeered) that as their "7 Mountain Mandate" - but with decidedly "kingdom now dominionism" marching orders for the Manifest Sons of God and Joel's Army. The NAR emphasizes taking down evil strongholds, binding Satan and demons, while retaking these seven societal institutions as the pre-requisite for releasing Jesus to return from heaven.

Nothing New Under The Sun

Ecclesiastes 1:9 is profoundly true about today's NAR. *"That which has been is that which will be, and that which has been done is that which will be done, so there is nothing new under the sun"*. History shows that all kinds of false teachers started with a "new" and special revelation given by an angel, visions, dreams, or the audible voice of God. Muhammad (7th Century) claimed the angel Gabriel gave him a "new" revelation superior to the canon of the Old and New Testaments. Joseph Smith (1830) said the angel Maroni showed him where to dig up the Book of Mormon, which was a "new" and more complete revelation than the Bible. Ellen White (1850s) said she was regularly visited by an "accompanying angel" while her 200 visions imparted "new" insights about the Bible as she founded the 7th Day Adventists. Charles Taze Russell started publishing the Watchtower (1879) stating Jesus was actually the archangel Michael. That same year, Mary Baker Eddy started Christian Science based on her visions and experiences for supernatural healings. Both Sun Myung Moon

(Unification Church in 1954) and Jim Jones (People's Temple in 1955) claimed they were the second coming of Jesus Christ. And the list goes on and on, from David Koresh and Marshall Applewhite, to Yahweh ben Yahweh and Alan John Miller. In each case, these false teachers, prophets, apostles, and messiahs all purported to have a "new" revelation that superseded what is in the Bible.

The NAR is yet another "new" global movement of false apostles and prophets perpetuating a re-packaged spiritual deception built upon their own experiences with miracles, signs, and wonders. However, the Bible is clear that Apostles (there still are only twelve) were chosen in person by Jesus. Peter, Andrew, James and John the sons of Zebedee, Philip, Thomas, Matthew, James the son of Alpheus, Thaddeus, Simon, and Bartholomew were the eleven men remaining after Judas Iscariot's betrayal and death. While Matthias was chosen by these eleven casting lots, there is no other mention of him as an Apostle because Saul of Tarsus was personally chosen by Jesus as the 12th Apostle (Acts 9, Galatians 1:11-12). Paul later stayed 15 days in Jerusalem with fellow Apostle Peter and Jesus' brother James (Galatians 1:18-19). On his second trip there, he took Barnabas and Titus to present to Peter, James, and John his message of the Gospel to the Gentiles (Galatians 2:1-2). They fully extended their hands of fellowship confirming Paul as an Apostle. In addition, Revelation 21:14 clearly confirms there are, and always will be, only 12 Apostles.

The Bible has an insightful principle about these so called "new" apostles in our contemporary world - they are *"boastful"* in their self-elevation, *"desiring to be regarded equal alongside the original and true twelve Apostles"* chosen by Jesus; however, *"such men are false apostles, deceitful workers, disguising themselves as apostles of Christ"* (2nd Corinthians 11:12-13). Paul had to deal with these same kinds of men and women coming into the churches in Corinth, Rome, Ephesus, Galatia, Colossae, Thessalonica, and Philippi. Peter also dealt with similar false teachers trying to enter into the church of Jerusalem and throughout Judea. So it should come as no surprise that the same type of men and women would be active once again in and around Calvary Chapel. The NAR and *entertaining deception* is not unique to the 21st Century church. There are over three dozen verses in the New Testament dealing with deception, false teachers, false doctrine, false messiahs-prophets-apostles, counterfeit Christs, doctrines of demons, Satan disguised as an angel of light, wolves disguised as sheep in the church, and the need to hold fast to sound doctrine.

You now have an overview of the NAR as a global movement built on the foundational principles of replacement theology. The next chapter examines specific cases of how those in the NAR practice signs and wonders that are in various ways and forms now starting to show up in Calvary Chapel churches, sometimes subtly, and other times quite prominently.

CHAPTER FOUR
Signs and Wonders

Seeing Is Believing

This topical heading has a double meaning [much like the book's title] because the NAR places such a premium on having to SEE God, or meet and speak with Jesus in person in order to truly believe. One has to SEE His power at work, SEE the glory come down from heaven, SEE the presence manifested, such that for the NAR "seeing" is now paramount to belief, even though there's a strong Biblical basis for not having to literally "see" God or Jesus or the Spirit face-to-face in order to believe and be satisfied in knowing Him. But whether in person at an NAR event, conference, or church service, or in photos online, in magazines, and in books, watching a DVD, television broadcast, online course, web podcast, or YouTube video, you will literally have to "see to believe" for yourself what those in the NAR do, say, and sing. Whether shaking, screaming, convulsing, barking, howling, dancing, meditating, chanting, jumping, bending, falling, applauding, or mumbling - these supposed signs and wonders from God are what the NAR seeks after as tangible confirmation that the Holy Spirit is moving in one's life. Those in the NAR regularly speak of their movement as superior to the "typical Christian life in America" that lacks special signs of God's presence. Yet the Bible simply says *"Don't you know that your body is now a temple of the Holy Spirit who is in you, whom you have from God?"* (1st Corinthians 6:19-20). The greatest miracle we have is that the Holy Spirit resides in us, and we can exhibit the fruit of His Spirit in our daily lives.

This fixation and over-emphasis on seeking after tangible signs and wonders paves the way for the *entertaining deception* that Christians should manifest daily supernatural evidences of: 1) speaking in tongues to commune directly with God in the "language of heaven"; 2) receiving special words from God all day and passing them to friends, family, co-workers, neighbors, and especially people at church, as evidence of God's presence; 3) prophesying "new" messages from God about world events and the church, as God supposedly amplifies and expands upon what is already clearly found in the Bible; 4) having supernatural faith to believe God for health and material blessings of wealth and prosperity as confirmations of His pleasure; 5) the ability to recognize the activity and "mischief" of demons and dark forces in the world all through the day, and to rebuke them, bind them, and cast them back into hell; 6) enacting the power of God daily through supernatural, miraculous signs and wonders that demonstrate God at work in you; and 7) invoking God's presence many times each day as the tangible sign He is supernaturally nearby.

To be very clear, of course God still does miracles in the lives of people as He exercises His sovereign will and providential care over creation. Pastors and elders throughout Calvary Chapels have always laid hands on those who were sick, anointing them with oil, and praying for God to heal if it's His will to do so - all in obedience to the sound doctrine shown in Genesis 48, Hebrews 6, Matthew 8, Mark 1, Luke 4, Acts 9, and of course James 5. During my 33 years at Calvary Costa Mesa and Calvary Santa Barbara, including missions trips, outreach concerts, men's retreats, afterglows, prayer team, and five years on the elder board with Pastor Ricky Ryan, I have seen first-hand how God answers prayer in extraordinary ways to accomplish His will. I have seen and heard physician exams that medically verified physical healings in people for whom we prayed. I have prayed and fasted on decisions facing the church, and watched first-hand how the Lord directed, guided, and provided beyond all we could ever ask or think. And I have experienced God's Holy Spirit empowering people for spiritual equipping during outreach to those with no knowledge of the gospel. But there is NO Biblical basis requiring God to do miraculous signs and wonders to confirm Himself in our lives. In fact, the greatest miracle is that God's Spirit abides in us as the down payment on our redemption, and we can exhibit His fruit - love, joy, peace, patience, kindness, goodness, faithfulness, gentleness, and self-control. Not of ourselves, but Him living through us.

I have regularly been asked by those who are pursuing signs, wonders, and the teachings of various false prophets and apostles, "Hey, Dr. Dave, does God speak to you?" and of course I know the underlying direction they want to take our conversation, so I always love to reply with, "Yes, all the time", which immediately piques their interest as they smile and say, "Tell us about that". But just as quickly as their eyes and ears perked up to my initial "Yes", their countenance drops as I explain, "Every time I read God's Word, the Lord speaks directly to me and gives me exactly what I need right then". A similar thing happens when folks ask, "Well then, does God still do miracles?" and of course my reply is always, "Absolutely" and when they want the details, I first tell them, "Why just this past week, five people came forward at church to put their faith in Jesus Christ, and I had the privilege to pray with one young man and see the incredible miracle of how the Lord changed his heart through forgiveness, mercy, and grace". They hoped to hear fantastic stories of me hearing audible voices, being transported to heaven, healing people, raising the dead, casting out demons, or calling angels to assist me on a mission outreach.

Remember this. Dispensational theology believes special works of God were provided only to the First Century Apostles - in that dispensation [of time] to support the launch and initial growth of the Church. Those miraculous gifs then ceased once the Apostles died and the Church had established a strong footing across the Roman world. Classic Pentecostal theology not only embraces those special works of God as still valid for today, but requires that certain of these spiritual gifts are the confirming evidence of God's Spirit in a true believer. Calvary Chapel has always struck the wonderful balance in these two positions - as Pastor Chuck noted in his book *Living Water,* the Holy Spirit dwells WITH us (*"para"* in the Greek, meaning that counselor who comes alongside us); He also dwells IN us (the Greek preposition *"en"*), and He can also come UPON us ("epi") "to empower the believer for service - an outflowing of the Spirit". He continues: *"The overarching principle concerning the gifts of the Spirit is this: the true gifts, when manifested in a scriptural and correct way will always focus people on Jesus Christ . . . or is there a great deal of attention drawn to the person exercising the gift?"*

Remember also the clear deception that signs and wonders constitute "seeing is believing" for the Christian life. Jesus stated very clearly in Matthew 16 to those wanting Him to perform a supernatural sign for them, *"A wicked and perverse generation seeks after signs, but I tell you this, only one sign shall be given to you, the sign of Jonah, for as Jonah was 3 days and 3 nights in the belly of the fish, so too the Son of Man shall be 3 days and 3 nights in the heart of the earth".* Do you realize what Jesus is saying? There is just ONE sign necessary for us, and that's Jesus' resurrection from the dead, for having been crucified "Jesus died for our sins ACCORDING TO THE SCRIPTURES, and then He was buried and raised from the dead on the third day ACCORDING TO THE SCRIPTURES" [1st Corinthians 15]. If a person had no other miraculous sign than that, it alone is entirely sufficient as THE defining sign of assurance from God. Jesus also clarified, "Blessed are those who have NOT seen me, and yet believe" (John 20). And finally, we are reminded that while God used to speak to His people "through prophets in many portions and many ways" [Hebrews 1], "He has now spoken to us directly by His Son", and we have today God's very Word (the Logos) detailed in the Bible, so that we lack nothing when it comes to knowing about and hearing from God.

The following sections cover signs and wonders in the contemporary NAR, organized in four groupings. First, those dealing with physical LOCATION, second what PEOPLE DO, third how PEOPLE INTERACT, and fourth how these enter into WORSHIP ministry. There's a LOT here to cover, so here we go.

THE CHURCH FACILITY

Tabernacle Of David - Waiting For The Presence

We previously noted that replacement theology is a foundational component of the NAR. This shows up where accounts in the Old Testament specifically describing God's interaction with Israel have now become the "new" way for Christians to have a fuller, more Biblically accurate relationship with God.

The NAR loves to model worship services after what they say is the true model for worship shown in Israel's portable tent of meeting in the wilderness [and later, the Temple in Jerusalem]. This "Tabernacle of David" principle says that just like the Hebrews waited on Yahweh to show His arrival and "presence" in the tabernacle, He now does the same thing in the contemporary Christian church. The sanctuary fills with earnest, expectant believers and they worship, yearn, plead, desire, long after, and wait for God to show Himself as having arrived and visited His people by filling the sanctuary with a tangible sign of His "presence". The worship might have to go on for an hour, maybe even longer, in order to get God to finally show His presence as His people cry out for . . .

Heaven Come Down

The NAR is fixated on bringing heaven down to earth. They continue to recount their visions, dreams, and spiritual trips to heaven as an additional seal on their Apostolic-Prophetic experiences with God - something all Christians should aspire to. In the same way that Ezekiel, Isaiah, and John bar-Zebedee each saw the heavenly scene, the NAR Apostles and Prophets preach countless hours of sermons, podcasts, and YouTube videos babbling on and on about summoning heaven to come down to earth. NAR Apostle Rodney Howard-Browne infamously states in his 1992 book *Fresh Oil From Heaven* that in 1979 he gave God an ultimatum: "either you come down here and touch me, or I am going to come up there and touch you". There are also dozens of NAR worship lyrics that speak about Jesus bringing heaven down to earth, or God's people yearning for heaven to descend. None of these concepts or images are Biblical. In fact when Peter, James, and John witnessed the transfiguration of Jesus, they could hardly bear seeing just a glimpse of His glory. God is present with believers ALWAYS through His Holy Spirit so there is no need for heaven (which is outside of time-space) to be brought into our temporal world here on earth.

Glory Cloud - Gold Dust

Linked directly to that Tabernacle of David and signs of His presence, the NAR boasts a supposedly "new" work of God in sending a cloud of glory direct from heaven that descends onto church attendees during worship and prayer. Not a fog or mist like in the Bible, it's now fine particles of gold dust settling on everyone like a gentle snowfall. The videos of such depict everyone screaming, applauding, and crying in complete amazement as the flakes land on their hair, clothing, seats, and outstretched hands. A colleague of mine with a PhD in chemistry explained that gold has a melting point of 1,948°F - yet the videos show the gold particles smearing as people touch the thin accumulation. So either this gold is at the liquefied temperature of nearly 2,000°F (which would scorch skin, clothes, hair), or just maybe it's actually finely atomized gold paint sprayed through the HVAC system. It's worth noting there's not a single instance of verifying this "gold dust" with a chemist or gemologist [especially intriguing considering that gold currently trades at around $1,300 an ounce]. It's very interesting that the Bible clearly teaches the lack of eternal value gold has when compared with wisdom, righteousness, and a sound heart and mind [see 1st Peter 1:7, Psalm 19:10, Matthew 10:9, Acts 17:29, 1st Peter 1:18, Acts 3:6, James 5:3, and Matthew 23:16-17]. Remember this, we have not been bought with perishable things from the earth - like gold. Enough said.

Angel Feathers

The NAR also has a fascination with angels. Seeing them, hearing their wings flap (really?), communing with them - even praying to or calling upon them. Many now claim that after the worship they find angel feathers on the floor, seats, or their clothing. Like the gold dust glory-cloud, there is absolutely NO Biblical basis for this. Videos of people holding these with trembling hands are entirely false because first, like the gold dust, no one has had one of these feathers analyzed to verify it did not come from any earthly bird. Would not the DNA have to be other than animal or human? Second, in the Bible, angels tell people they should not be exalted [Revelation 22:8-9], and in God's creation, mankind is *"a little lower than then angels"* [Hebrews 2], so they are also created beings who serve the Lord as we do; and they are described as having "an appearance of a man" - they DON'T HAVE WINGS and FEATHERS [Genesis

18:2 *"Abraham saw three men standing there"*; Luke 1:26 the angel speaks to Mary; Acts 12:5 the angel led Peter from prison; Acts 8:26 an angel spoke to Philip]. People confuse angels with Seraphim [Isaiah 6] in heaven who cover themselves with what look like wings, and Cherubim [Exodus 25] with wings touching on the Ark of the Covenant. Too many Christians believe in angel wings from movies like John Travolta as *Michael*, Tilda Swinton in *Constantine*, Paul Bettan in *Legion*, or Clarence getting wings by helping George Baily. Matthew Ward's 1979 "Toward Eternity" album cover had a rock band comprised of winged angels. Some embrace the chubby toddler variety angel with little wings in Renaissance art. But be reminded that *"by showing kindness to strangers, many of us have entertained angels without even knowing"* [Hebrews 13:2], so they have the appearance of a man [Daniel 10:5], and don't have wings.

Diamonds And Jewels

NAR worship services claim another tangible sign of God being present is finding diamonds and other jewels after the service. Like gold dust and angel feathers, there is no Biblical basis for this. God's Word teaches that wisdom is more precious than jewels [Proverbs 8:11], as is a godly woman [Proverbs 3:15, 31:10]. There is no Biblical account of this as a model, and once again, it would be nice to have a jeweler-gemologist verify such props shown on

YouTube videos. Be reminded that Lucifer was the one described as being covered ornately with every kind of jewel and precious gem [see Ezekiel 28].

WHAT PEOPLE DO

Slain In The Spirit

NAR services always have people come to the front for prayer and then by a touch to the forehead, a wave of the hand, or even blowing onto the face by the pastor, prophet, or apostle, the person collapses backward into the waiting arms of attendants who gently lay them down to the floor. This is being "slain in the spirit" - a supposedly clear sign of the Holy Spirit coming over a person. Supporters often point to how the Roman guards at Jesus' tomb fell back like dead men as the angel rolled away the stone, or how Ananias and Sapphira fell back when confronted by Peter. These Biblical accounts always astound me as the Roman guardians were NOT believers waiting on the Holy Spirit's presence [Matthew 28:4], and Ananias and Sapphira were struck down dead (not "as dead") because they lied to the Holy Spirit [Acts 5]. These are in no way models for believers being slain in (receiving) the Holy Spirit.

Drunk In The Spirit

The NAR teaches that believers can be "drunk" in God's Holy Spirit, but this has two obvious and significant flaws. First, the Holy Spirit is a Person. He is God in the well-documented Biblical doctrine of our Triune God. The Spirit is

NOT a force, an aura, or mystical trance that comes over an individual. Second, the Bible clearly teaches to NOT be drunk, as with wine [Ephesians 5:18]. The NAR describes how people "lose control" or are "completely overwhelmed" when "overcome" by the Spirit (like alcohol). Some call it a "WUI" (worshipping under the influence), like a felony "DUI". Really? The Bible teaches we are instead to be filled with the Holy Spirit as the exact opposite of being drunk because we are still very much conscious and aware of what's happening, and retain remembrance of such. NAR Apostle Rodney Howard-Browne has multiple online sermons and podcasts where he openly calls upon the "Holy Ghost Bartender" to start distributing "the good wine" on the people, calling out "let's set 'em up again and do another round" as if the Holy Spirit is dispensed like booze at a nightclub. Then comes the shaking, convulsing, yelling hysterically - certainly these are NOT evidences of a sound mind in the Holy Spirit, but more like the description of the man in Genessaret possessed by multiple demons. Yet Kansas City Prophet Paul Cain supports this crazy behavior, stating: "*God will offend the mind to reveal the heart, [the issue] is one of control, [as] God wants to know who among His people is willing to play the fool for His glory*". That man tormented by demons was later clothed, controlled, and in his right mind AFTER Jesus freed him. And remember, Paul clearly states the work of the Holy Spirit is not confusion, but always done in order [1st Corinthians 14:33].

Toking The Ghost

It's not enough be slain by God's Spirit, or to be drunk on God's Spirit, as if imbibed like beer, wine, or liquor to a point of being inebriated and losing control of one's faculties. NAR Prophets and Apostles also use the pop-culture terminology for smoking marijuana ("toking") to describe people getting "high on the Holy Spirit" - calling it "Jehovah-juana" to convey that Christians should want more and more of the Spirit to get as spiritually "high" as possible. This is a complete disrespecting of God's Spirit, aligning 1st Corinthians 6:19-20 with smoking pot. It is also an entirely unbiblical premise that Christians might not get ALL of the Holy Spirit they need, or expect - that somehow God has held out on them from His fullest degree of filling or indwelling - requiring believers to exercise their own form of "toking" (begging, pleading, yearning) in order to get that fullest measure of God's Spirit, and achieve that maximum "high". The Bible is clear, we have received ALL we need from God's Holy Spirit: Psalm 23 "we shall not want"; James 1:4 we are then "perfected and complete, lacking in nothing"; and 1st Corinthians 1:7 we "lack nothing in any spiritual gifting".

Spiritual Re-Birthing And Nursing

You might have thought slain in, drunk with, and toking the Holy Spirit represented the lowest points to which someone could reduce God. But once again "seeing is believing". Many hyper-charismatic NAR worship and healing services, as well as unbiblical counseling sessions, encourage people to be "spiritually re-birthed" - laying on their backs, their legs are spread as they claim to experience birthing pains, and re-enact how a woman pushes her baby down the birth canal. This is supposedly highly symbolic of being born again to new life, and is often followed up immediately with spiritual "nursing from El-Shaddai", or "lying on the breast of Jesus" (alluding to John at the last supper). However, Jesus told Nicodemus that a person does NOT go back into the womb for re-birthing in order to be born again [John 3:1-21]. "True milk of the Word" [1st Peter 2:2] has absolutely nothing to do with believers figuratively breast-feeding from God.   Let me simply say that the online videos and audio teachings on this are the most ridiculous purported expressions of seeing God's Spirit act in a person's life that the NAR prophets and apostles have concocted.

Toronto Blessing - Holy Laughter

But wait, I may have spoken too soon. The Toronto Airport Vineyard church was considered THE destination-hub of supernatural signs and spiritual wonders during 1994 when a supposedly "new" work of God's Holy Spirit was manifest in the lives of the pastors, staff, and attendees. Under the direction of husband and wife co-pastors John and Carol Arnott, people were supposedly so overwhelmed by the Holy Spirit that they began to bark like dogs and howl like wolves. In time, that proceeded to uncontrollable, hysterical "holy laughter".

But Romans 8:9 says do NOT be in the flesh with such ridiculous exhibitions - and 1st Corinthians 12 describes the orderly way the Holy Spirit administers His spiritual gifts when the church assembles, why? - so that unbelievers will not think you are like some sort of drunk who has obviously lost all control.

Spiritual Teleportation

The NAR focuses on personally experiencing heaven, as dozens of their Prophets and Apostles claim they have regular access to heaven, to visit and speak with Jesus and 1st Century Apostles. Jason Westerfield, whose 2008 book *"God Come To Me Or I'm Coming To You"* (Messianic Visions Publishers) tells how he travels in a "spiritual manner" up into heaven to speak with Jesus, Adam, Old Testament prophets and other Apostles, and how he has been invisibly transported to the White House where he sat in on meetings without anyone knowing he was there (that's always convenient). In his book, he admonishes all readers to follow his simple teachings to learn his "techniques" on how to do the exact same thing. This is just plain silly.

A "New" Name

One common practice is for NAR Apostles and Prophets to tell people it's important to learn your "new" name, using an out-of-context distortion of Revelation 2:17 where Jesus told the Pergamum church "*to him who overcomes I will give a white stone and new name written on it no one knows*". The idea is that this elevates one's relationship with God to learn your "new" name from Jesus while still on earth. I know several accounts of Calvary men's or women's retreats where people go on a hike and are instructed to find a stone, hold it tightly, and ask the Lord to reveal their "new name", then write it on the stone. People get so excited and feel extra "special" that they can now commune with God using their new name. How sad they don't remember solid Bible study from the retreat, but instead now carry around - and revere - that stone.

DISCIPLESHIP

Spiritual Fathering - Shepherding

The NAR also advocates a "new" form of personal advocacy between Christians who are less mature in their walk with God, and the spiritually mature (elite) believers who visit and see God in heaven, and work miracles, signs, and wonders. This latter person becomes the "spiritual parent" to the other as the "spiritual father" - going to God on the other's behalf, then coming back to relay God's instructions about life decisions and important matters. This is the role performed by priests in various orthodoxy, who go-between for average parishioners unable see and hear God on their own. Also called "shepherding", the elite Christian with direct access to God guides and instructs others in all manners of decision making: where to attend school, what job to take, where to live, whom to marry, how to manage finances. But 1st Timothy 2:5 clearly says, *"there is one God, and one mediator also between God and men, Christ Jesus"*.

Yet various organizations offer programs, certificates, and even formal educational degrees in Spiritual Fathering, Shepherding, or being a Spiritual Guide. Here are examples. The *World Coach Institute* in Key Largo, FL offers a Certified Spiritual Coach (CSC) degree. *Life Mastery Institute* in Westlake Village, CA offers courses for the designation of Spiritual Life Coach (SLC). *Divine Intelligence Institute* in Allen, TX has an SLC certificate to support others in "awakening the God within". *Holistic Learning Centers* offer online SLC courses to "Learn to coach like [Deepak] Chopra, and (Marianne) Williamson". Lynda Dyer from *Evolve Now* is a nationally known archetypal spiritual guide offering programs to unlock inner spiritual portals to the divine. *Inner Visions Institute for Spiritual Development* in Maryland boasts it is "the only known credentialing institution for the SLC (yet I found two dozen others in a Google search). Right here in Santa Barbara, *Pacifica Graduate Institute* has Masters degrees in archetypal Depth Psychology "based on **personal** experience of the sacred, avoiding all forms of doctrine and dogma", while a local "wellness center" provides spiritual fathering, dream interpretation, and regressive-counseling under the direction of people who worked with Mike Bickle's Kansas City House of Prayer and John Paul Jackson's Streams Ministries. What do these centers and institutes ALL have in common? Men and women from Calvary Chapel churches have attended/graduated from these programs, and are actively involved in these false doctrines and unbiblical practices, even as they continue to attend their local Calvary Chapel church.

Grave-Soaking

It has become very popular among youth and college groups in the NAR to take "pilgrimages" to the graves of famous Christians for the purpose of absorbing remnants of the residual spirituality, vision, gifting, and passion for the Gospel from dead saints. People lay down prostrate on the grave, close their eyes, and pray that the Lord would supernaturally infuse them, equip, and transfer to them the power and calling that the deceased person had in life during their earthly ministry. Whether kneeling on Martin Luther's grave at All Saints Church in Wittenberg, Germany - lying on the floor of Wesley Chapel in London - spreading out on the grass in front of the headstone for D.L. Moody in Northfield, Massachusetts - or embracing the sepulcher of John Calvin in Geneva, Switzerland, grave-soaking (also called grave-sucking) falsely offers spiritually immature and undiscerning seekers a "new" type of meta-connection inspiration with famous Christians from years gone by. This is like a séance, where the living try to contact the dead to gain special knowledge or powers from beyond the grave. In 1st Samuel 28 the distressed King Saul, who no longer heard from the Lord, sought out a spiritual conjurer to call up the spirit of the dead prophet Samuel to get some counsel. That can never be a basis to support grave soaking. This reminds me of how my wife's French-language students from Santa Barbara High used to visit Jim Morrison's grave during our annual Spring Break trip to Paris, believing a form of inspiration was present from the Doors' lead singer who died in 1971. I laugh out loud remembering the comedy film "This Is Spinal Tap", where band members make a pilgrimage to Graceland and can't get their a-cappella harmonies on "Heartbreak Hotel" to work as they try to gain inspiration at the grave of Elvis. While that is comical, the idea that Christians today would seek residual spiritual "energy" at a grave, to be soaked in through physical proximity, is truly tragic. The Bible teaches either a person dies and then the judgment [Hebrews 9:27], or a true believer is absent from the body and present with the Lord [2nd Corinthians 5:8]. My final comment is simply that Jesus stated in his rebuke of the pompous, self-righteous religious leaders, that they were as white-washed tombs - clean and ornate on the outside, but inside, full of dead men's bones. So, enough said as to whether there is any truth in the clearly un-Biblical practice of grave soaking.

Dream Interpretation

Many in the NAR are fixated on God speaking to them through fantastic dreams. This gets back to Joel 2:28 - desiring to be son and daughters who dream dreams and see visions - the Manifest Sons of God, Joel's Army. NAR prophets and apostles have created courses about HOW to interpret dreams, based on Jungian humanistic archetypal psychology and "primers", while wrongly linked to two Biblical accounts: Daniel's interpreting Nebuchadnezzar's dream, and Joseph's dream about his family. Yet neither of these accounts was provided for believers as a template through which the meanings of ALL dreams can be known. In both cases, the dream interpretation was given by God - not figured out by Daniel or Joseph using an archetype rubric. Perhaps the most infamous false teacher in this area was the late NAR super-Apostle John Paul Jackson, founder of Texas-based Streams Ministries. He created an elaborate archetypal "mapping" system, with categories of images, sounds, and places supposedly common in all dreams, and how to master the ability to interpret spiritual meaning in these. This all hinged on the underlying premise that he had exceptional spiritual powers and insights from his "special" and direct communion with God, so he was uniquely qualified to pass along his scheme to others willing to sit at his feet and learn (and pay the course fees and purchase the books and other materials). Sad to say, men's and women's ministries, prayer ministries, and especially counseling ministries at some Calvary Chapels have begun to use such *entertaining deception,* as people look past God's Word for wisdom, knowledge, direction, guidance - and instead seek after special, fantastic, symbol-laden mystical dreams as God's way to guide and direct.

This is not to say that the Lord can't use a dream to communicate to a person. There are of course accounts of Christians having the Lord bring a word of knowledge through a dream for a very specific person or situation, and in these testimonies, the Lord's message was straightforward and clear, and the person knew what to do with this information. There are also numerous accounts of those in Muslim nations (with no access to a Bible), having dreams where Jesus comes and clearly explains the Gospel and they accept Him as their savior. Both of these examples have not required another person to interpret the dream using a man-made curriculum of archetype symbols. Instead, the dream was a plain and simple message that did not require interpretation.

Tattoo And Piercing Interpretation

Another disconcerting extension of the prior dream-interpretation signs and wonders is the supposedly insightful prophecies to be interpreted in the tattoos and piercings on people's bodies. About an hour north of here in Santa Maria, an NAR would-be Prophet offers online courses and in-person seminars to teach Christians how to interpret the "hidden prophetic messages behind tattoos and piercings", using his special knowledge for spiritual outreach in the world — ALL for just $79. His website notes that you can also watch the first course for free, but "this is a limited time offer". Again, sad to say, many college-age and young professionals have flocked to this NAR practice, believing God will impart special knowledge to them for the purpose of doing great signs and wonders that will help to bring Jesus back to earth.

Empaths And Intuitives

Perhaps the NAR is so overly focused on subduing the 7 Mountains that there's really nothing off limits in the New Age or humanistic psychology that cannot be co-opted into some form of sensational spiritual sign or wonder. Just south of here in the mountain enclave of Ojai, CA - two infamous NAR Apostles have offered seminars on "How To Unlock Your Prophetic" and "How To Speak Into Other People's Lives". Similar courses have been taught in Santa Barbara and at retreat centers in the wine country of the Santa Ynez Valley. They bring in a "new" form of spiritual gifting referred to as being either an "Empath" or an "Intuitive" (obviously NOT gifts of the Holy Spirit from the Bible). The first is a shortened form of the word *empathy.* An Empath is spiritually endowed to listen to others tell of worries, cares, hurts, and then be able to miraculously empathize with them to both alleviate those anxieties, and transfer some of that pain over to the Empath who is trained to eliminate it for good. A person can initially explore if they "might be an Empath", and then learn how to develop that in the seminar. Dozens of Christians attend these, even those from local area Calvary Chapels, believing it provides a "new" discipleship tool for men's and women's ministries, as well pastoral and church counseling. Philippians 4 says, *"Be anxious for nothing, but in everything by prayer and supplication with thanksgiving, let all your requests be made known to God, and the peace of God which surpasses all human comprehension, will guard your hearts and your minds in Christ Jesus".* Unlike the Empath who hears the person tell of their sorrows, the Intuitive sits quietly with a person, they say nothing, and through supernatural intuition are able to perceive what a person feels. This is nothing more than attempts at traditional New Age extra sensory perception (ESP) and is more a parlor game or stage show than any kind of Biblical gifting.

WORSHIP

Singing In The Spirit

Watch videos of many contemporary NAR worship leaders and bands on the web, or attend a "special anointed" praise and worship service at some church, concert hall, or sports venue, and this typically includes the NAR phenomenon 'Singing in the Spirit'. Separate from the regular congregational singing, the worship leader and musicians break from leading people in worship as the lyrics on the screen go dark and everyone is now watching, applauding, and aspiring to the special anointed communion shown as the worship leader moves into a free-form meandering of impromptu melodies and lyrics that is a "higher" form of worship - direct from the Holy Spirit, unique from the song-set all were singing previously. The first problem with this is that it halts the congregation's worship as everyone stops, stands, and stares at the worship leader perform a solo act that can last for several minutes. Second, it sets the worship leader on a podium of how a truly spirit-filled believer worships at a higher, spontaneous, and intimate level - with the Holy Spirit now singing "new" music and lyrics through that anointed person. And third, the focus and attention moves away from the Lord, with the audience now enamored at "how amazing the worship leader is". Read Ezekiel 28 and Isaiah 14 to get a Biblical view of a worship leader who turned the focus away from God and on himself.

Waiting For The Presence

Back again to the Tabernacle of David - where Christians are like Israel coming to wait for a physical sign that God's Spirit would descend from heaven and be manifested through the smoke that would fill that space, NAR worship leaders and song lyrics focus on "inviting the Spirit" to come, "waiting for the presence" to show up, asking for ":heaven to come", calling down "the fire" to fall, "yearning to see your glory", and telling God "we're desperate". These all have two core flaws. First, those are Old Testament figures/images from a time when the Holy Spirit did not dwell richly in the hearts of believers, as He does now. And second, with God's Spirit living in our hearts full-time, there's no need to invite or call on Him to show up at worship services. He's already present! The New Testament clearly teaches: *"now He who establishes us in Christ and anoints us is God, who seals us by giving us the Holy Spirit in our hearts as a pledge"* (1st Corinthians 1:21-22) and *"having also believed, you were sealed in Him with the Holy Spirit of promise given as a pledge of our inheritance, with a view to the [future] redemption [of us] as God's very own possession"* (Ephesians 1:13-14). The Holy Spirit does not have to be invited to attend church, and we don't have to wait on (and hope for) Him to show up. Perhaps it's most important to remember that "God does not dwell in houses built by human hands" [Acts 7:48 and Acts 17:24] - but in the hearts of believers.

HIGHER PRAYER

Sozo Prayer

Many Calvary Chapels have begun contemplative prayer techniques that originate in the godless practices of Jungian depth psychology (visualization, archetypes, role-play), Eastern mysticism (transcendental meditation, relaxation methods, and repetitive mantras), or supposedly more "Christian" models from the monastics and other "holiness" traditions. Sozo prayer [Greek for "deliver"] was concocted by husband-wife co-pastors Bill and Beni Johnson of Bethel Church. They allege it's "a unique inner healing and deliverance ministry in which the main focus is to get to the root of those things hindering your personal connection with the Father, Son, and Holy Spirit." Issues that supposedly reside in subconscious memories are named out loud as a person is regressed through guided imagery and suggestions by a Sozo therapist. *Berean Call* notes that "this is nothing more than spiritualized psychotherapy, using occult techniques and methodologies".

Centering Prayer

The NAR is also active in teaching and promoting "centering prayer" as superior to the average everyday prayer of "common" Christians. It's all about a quasi transcendental meditation (TM) method where the person stays entirely focused on one word - or a few words [portions of a Bible verse] - and repeats that over and over like a chant or a mantra to supposedly clear the mind to hear more directly from God. The Bible teaches that we should pray with our minds [1st Corinthians 14:15], that we have clear 1-on-1 access with the Lord in simply speaking to God [Philippians 4:6]. It is not some "new" form of ritualistic mysticism that requires progressive steps or stages in order to get dialed into the right connection with God. Matthew 6:7 clearly teaches to not pray with vain repetitions, the way the heathen do. And when Paul said to "pray without ceasing" [1st Thessalonians 5:16-18], he did not mean babbling on and on without end. He clearly meant that believers can pray anytime and anywhere because there are no prerequisites that have to be followed in order to speak directly with the Lord. This carries over into the . . .

Lectio Divina

Another NAR prayer technique comes from Catholicism's Benedictine holiness tradition, the Lectio Divina (Latin for "Divine Word"). Using rhythmic breathing and slow, repetitive meditation-chanting of a Scripture verse over and over, a person must first prepare the mind before praying. But in Matthew 6:7 Jesus says, *"When you pray, do not use meaningless repetition as the Gentiles do, for they suppose that they will be heard for their many words"*. 'Gentiles' is the Greek ethnikos (ἐθνικός), also translated 'pagans'. Jesus also taught we should not pray like the religious leaders of his day, with all their rituals and pomp out in public for all to see how holy they are [Matthew 23], because they place heavy burdens (rituals) on others to adhere to endless requirements that place religious format over a personal relationship with God. Eight times he says "woe" (warning) to them and their exalted self-assessment, with the 7th being *"you hypocrites are like whitewashed tombs which on the outside appear beautiful, but inside are full of dead men's bones and uncleanness"*.

Kundalini Prayer

Another NAR "new" prayer method is adapted from the Hindu Kundalini - a form of meditative, transcendental yoga, where Christians use the 'Sa-Ta-

Na'Ma' (meaning "true identity" or "true divine") mantra and visualization to increase intuitive abilities and spiritual powers, clearing away negative emotions, traumas, and impressions that hinder the direct link to God. A person spends time trying to get the correct spinal alignment in place, from the hips to the brain, so there is a smooth energy flow to open the mind. Enough said!

Spiritual Formation

While most Christians who hear "spiritual formation" might understand that to be sanctification, where the Holy Spirit is continually maturing us as we grow in our knowledge and understanding of God's Word, the NAR defines it as something WE do by "raising the bar" (quoting Bill Johnson and Morris Cerrullo) through deliberate practices-methods raising us to "deeper consciousness", "closer to the level on which God exists". The late USC philosophy professor Dallas Willard's article 'Spiritual Formation' is often cited by the NAR as the basis for mapping-planning the kinds of activities we need to engage in to elevate our spirituality. *"We think spiritual formation [is] by the Holy Spirit; but not all by the Holy Spirit, [but] is done to us by those around us, by ourselves, and activities we voluntarily undertake"* [see dwillard.org]. In the NAR, it ends up being nothing more than a traditional system of self-help steps where people engage in daily visualizations of where they want to be, while speaking words-of-faith ("name it, claim it") aimed at attaining a higher spiritual life.

Confess Your Demons

One popular NAR false teaching is that the "true" believers' spiritual eyes must become open to the unseen spirit-world, to engage in daily battles, rebuking, binding, and confrontations with demons who are involved in every aspect of daily life - from various temptations and placing unclean thoughts into our minds, to causing problems for us at home and at work. Christians must come daily before the Lord and confess their demons (lust, anger, envy, over-eating, being upset with the kids), because every challenge a person runs into each day is a demon (or demons) hampering what we do. I know first-hand of a Calvary Chapel men's retreat where the guest speaker (a pastor from another Calvary) wrapped up his testimony about his own "battles with fear and doubt" by noting the Luke 8 account of the demon-possessed man in Gennesaret who "fell at the feet of Jesus". This pastor said it was a model for the 100+ men in the room to "do the same". As he asked the worship leader to come up front he said, "we'll now have time for men to come forward, fall at Jesus' feet, and confess your demons to the Lord". However, believers who have God's Spirit dwelling richly in them cannot be overcome by demons, demons do not plant thoughts in a Christian's mind, demons do not make us sin, and so we do not have demons that must be daily brought to the Lord and confessed. The story of the demon-possessed man is in no way a model for believers.

Learn How To . . .

The last areas include how the NAR has turned the "gifts" of the Holy Spirit - which are clearly described in God's Word as given by the Holy Spirit, as HE WILLS, for HIS purposes [1st Corinthians 12]- into skills or techniques that can be taught, tried out, and developed over time. These include courses on "How to heal", "How to prophesy", "How to have a word of knowledge", "How to speak in tongues", and "How to do miracles". The common thread is to take a class and learn the methodologies, then try it out to see how you do. Want to be a prophet? then first try it out to see if there might be something there, then keep practicing, during which "you might fire some blanks" early while in the development stage. International House of Prayer "healing rooms" not only are staffed with people who are healers, but they can also teach/train others to do the same. The core deception is that these "gifts" can be studied, practiced, and improved on over time. For example, I know several first-hand accounts of people being convinced by an NAR Apostle they had to bring sick friends and family members to Redding, CA to be cured in a Bethel "healing room". My counsel is always three logical things in light of Biblical truth. First, if these are truly Apostles, why don't THEY do the healing? Second, if this Apostle is part of a local House of Prayer, why not simply bring the friend to that HOP healing-room (why go to Redding)? And third (and most important), the Bible is clear that God is the ONLY one who heals, so could not the Lord simply heal the friend or family member with ordinary-average people praying for him?

A recent email from a popular NAR group claims "*there are three things Jesus said about how to cure disease*". It then offers "*try this Biblical health secret that has already been used by more than 10,270 Americans - the results they report are SHOCKING*". The embedded podcast entices people to learn a supposedly "forgotten passage in the Bible" where "*Jesus tells us exactly how to heal virtually any disease*". And of course it concludes with a blue web-link that says "Go watch it now before it's too late" — which sounds like a typical advertising promotion for a product coupon or rebate that's about to expire.

Summary

The NAR focus on signs are wonders covers a wide range of sensational practices, and there are many more than those covered here. The next chapter examines the relationship of personal experiences compared to God's Word.

CHAPTER FIVE
Experience vs. God's Word

The Central Problem

NAR Apostles and Prophets have one primary issue that undermines the entire movement. Their *entertaining deceptions* and false practices rest on the spiritually weak and shifting foundations of their own personal experiences that do not line up with sound Biblical doctrine. Pastor Chuck always taught that the Word of God is both precise in its details, and entirely sufficient in its depth and breadth of addressing all matters of spiritual life. He also reminded us that no doctrine, practice, or belief should be constructed from a single Bible verse, because God's Word is the very best commentary on God's Word, and will in all levels of its context always be confirming of sound doctrine, while exposing those ideas of men built out of context from just one Scripture verse. The NAR foundational doctrines covered in Chapter-3 ALL disregard the full context of the Bible, allowing for replacement theology, kingdom now dominionism, latter rain, manifest sons of God, Joel's army, bridal eschatology, and the 7-mountain mandate to define the lens through which modern day Apostles and Prophets view and understand God the Father, Jesus, the Holy Spirit, and the world. These then provide the underlying rationale that allows for the NAR practices noted in Chapter-4, from gold dust to angel feathers, grave-soaking to toking the Ghost, slain in the Spirit to Sozo-centered-contemplative prayer. Here in this chapter it's time to review how man's personal experiences should always be discerned relative to the Bible. The principle being that God's Word is ALWAYS the final authority on whether something from man is true or not.

The Precision of God's Word

The Bible is incredibly precise in its details and specific confirmations of dates, names, geography and countries, institutions, and sequence of events. The First Century A.D. was no doubt a very exciting time in the life of this new "Christian" movement that started in Judea, and then spread throughout the Mediterranean basin of the Roman Empire, and beyond. Jesus had entered Jerusalem April 6th in 32 A.D. - the 10th of Nisan on the Jewish calendar, the start of Passover. Scotland Yard's Sir Robert Anderson meticulously researched every issue and adjustment to the Hebrew, Julian, and Gregorian calendars, as per Daniel's mid-7th Century BC prophecy written during Israel's captivity in Babylon. It stated there would be 69 "weeks of years" (Jewish "Sha'bua" is one 7-year period) or 173,880 days *"from the edict to restore and rebuild Jerusalem until Messiah the king".* Persian Emperor Artaxerxes Longimanus issued that very declaration to Nehemiah on March 14th in 445 B.C. Inspector Anderson's precise calculations showed the first Sunday in April of 32 as THE DAY Jesus would ride into Jerusalem [Zechariah 9:9-17 and Matthew 21:1-11] and fulfill Daniel's prophecy to the exact day. In fact, Jesus intentionally waited until that specific time period was completed, even telling his followers in the prior days, weeks, months, and years when they wanted to proclaim Him publicly as the Messiah, that "My day has not yet come". Jesus was crucified four days later on Thursday April 10th - right on Passover (the 14th of Nisan) even as John the Baptist had precisely described Jesus as "the Lamb of God who takes away the sins of the world". He was resurrected after 3 days and 3 nights, so the tomb was empty on Sunday, April 13th - the 17th day of Nisan, which was both the anniversary of Noah's ark coming to rest on land again, and the Jewish Feast of Firstfruits. Fifty days later at the Feast of Pentecost in Jerusalem, God fulfilled His promise to send the Holy Spirit and the Church was born. There are over 380 verses from 28 different books of the Bible that consistently confirm events in history. This is also true for dozens of other Old Testament prophecies already clearly fulfilled. This kind of precision could not be by accident, and it was not because the Biblical authors had a meeting at a conference to coordinate their writing content. God's Word is a truly precise message with a supernatural origin outside our limited time-space perspective.

The Sufficiency of God's Word

The Bible is also 100% complete, needs no additional components, and lacks in nothing in order for God to effectively speak on all matters of truth. That early Church launch at Pentecost in late May of 32 A.D. did not have the complete Bible as we do today. But they did have a complete Old Testament in Greek (the Septuagint) for almost three centuries prior to Jesus' ministry. It provided those amazing details describing the coming of Messiah, his death, resurrection, and the sending of the Holy Spirit. Within just 35 years of Jesus' ministry, the four Gospels, Luke's Acts of the Apostles, the letters of Paul, Peter, James, John, and Jude – plus the Revelation of Jesus given to John on Patmos were all penned and being copied and circulated throughout the Mediterranean Basin as churches were launched in places like Rome, Corinth, Antioch, Ephesus, Philippi, Jerusalem, Galatia, Colossae, and Thessalonica. The complete canon of Scripture was in place by the 4th Century, and has endured through to the present 21st Century. God's Word is then entirely sufficient and a single source of truth, inspired by God, and profitable for these four things: *"teaching, reproof, correction, and training in righteousness, so that the man of God may be adequate, equipped for every good work"* [2nd Timothy 3:16-17]. We are truly blessed to have the Word of God be the basis for everything in the life of Calvary Chapel. However, some men and women don't see it that way.

The Variance of Personal Experience

The NAR places a huge (make that, HUGE) emphasis on one's personal "spiritual" experiences as being essentially on par with - and in some cases more important than - God's Word, regarding the weight and credibility given to visions, dreams, voices heard, miracles, feelings about situations, and of course supposed prophetic words and revelations received. These then become the bases for the "teachings" that false prophets and fake apostles do in their home churches, ministry organizations, and at conferences, concerts, and other special events. I have watched dozens of their YouTube and other online videos and podcasts, listened to their CDs and MP3s, and read a wide range of their books, magazine articles, blogs, and web postings. The false NAR Apostles and Prophets pronounce all kinds of wild, fantastic, miraculous claims about their own personal experiences that include: 1) traveling to heaven, 2) seeing Jesus, 3) talking with angels, 4) hearing God's voice, 5) doing signs and wonders, 5) speaking sensational words of prophecy, 6) healing all kinds of diseases, and 7) even raising people from the dead. They use these as the basis for their own unique "teachings" about God, Jesus, the Holy Spirit, evangelism, prophecy, and worship. But these don't qualify as a Biblical message, because the emphasis is on what they've supposedly seen, heard, said, and done - their personal "special" revelations - while giving little, if any, reference to God's Word in its full context of sound doctrine.

God's Word Confirms Either Way

Deuteronomy 4:2 clearly warns, *"Don't add to the Word, and don't subtract from the Word"*. In Matthew 24:32 Jesus declares that *"heaven and earth shall pass away, but God's Word shall never pass away"*. And we're reminded in 2nd Peter 1:20-21 that *"no prophecy of scripture ever comes by the person's own imagination, for no prophecy is ever carried by a human impulse"*. So when Mike Bickle (IHOP-Kansas City) tells how his leg started shaking in the middle of the night before he went flying through the roof at fantastic speed to heaven where he spoke with Jesus and angels, and then came zooming back to his bedroom, this becomes the sole basis for his teachings, as he then self-validates the "new" revelations he claims he heard. But the more important issue is whether these fantastic tales and special words line up with what we already know to be true in God's Word. The same holds true for John Paul Jackson's stories of walking through caves in his dreams and encountering demonic forces, animals, displays of light, and angels with "new" messages about visions and prophetic words. Bill Johnson, Lou Engle, Patricia King, Paul Cain, Heidi Baker, and Todd Bentley ramble on about "secrets" they have received from God in visions or Sozo prayer. Their videos and books are filled with hundreds of personal experiences about: angels in warrior gear with "new" instructions to prepare Joel's Army, "new" chapters for the Bible that were kept secret in heaven until being released now, Satan being bound by prophetic words, and special anointed instructions direct from God about "new" ways to pray, worship, meditate, and be overwhelmed by the "Presence".

In *Charisma vs. Charismania,* Pastor Chuck reminds us that when a person stands up in the middle of a Sunday morning service while the sermon is being taught and starts speaking in tongues or declaring supposed prophecy, it's easy to simply remember 1st Corinthians 12, that everything is to be done in order by the leading of the Holy Spirit, and ask "If the pastor is teaching God's Word by the leading of the Holy Spirit, why then would the Holy Spirit interrupt Himself through that person who stood up and started talking out loud?" For all those in Calvary Chapel churches, it's just as easy to simply lay any and all personal spiritual experiences they read or hear about right up against the sound doctrine found in God's Word. The Bible will always prove to be both precise and sufficient to judge and discern what's true and what's false.

For example, the reason we can clearly recognize replacement theology as not being sound doctrine is because all the Old Testament prophecies about Messiah's first coming were literally fulfilled by Jesus. And those prophecies about Israel being re-gathered back into the land from the four corners of the earth, with the desert bringing forth its agricultural bounty, and Jerusalem being restored to the nation have also been literally fulfilled since 1948. So it's then entirely consistent to believe that the yet unfulfilled prophecies about Israel and the Messiah will also happen literally in a still future time period.

Without the Word of God as a final authority, people follow their own ideas, thoughts, and commentary on spiritual matters, gifting, church life, prophecy - and gradually drift away from the timeless truths in God's Word. Psalm 119:87 states: *"Forever, O Lord, your Word is settled in heaven"*, while verse 160 says *"The sum of your Word is truth"*. The angelic visitations with "new" revelations purported by Mohammed and Joseph Smith are easy to discern as false because Galatians 1:8 teaches *"if we, or even if an angel from heaven preaches to you a gospel contrary to what we preached to you, he is to be accursed"*. Mary Baker Eddy's personal experiences with hypnotism, dreams, and clairvoyance - or Charles Taze Russell's vision that Christ returned to earth invisibly and the 144,000 are not the twelve tribes of Israel, are easily identified as false because sound doctrine does not support these experiences. Similar personal escapades of NAR Apostles and Prophets that sound sincere when wrapped in emotions with terms like "glory" and "presence", are easily discerned when they find no support in the full counsel of God's Word. The next chapter explains the common ways that deception enters into the church.

CHAPTER SIX
How Deception Enters In

Knocking At The Door

The deceptions and false teachings of the NAR have come right up to the door of Calvary Chapel (and hundreds of other churches) and knocked to see if anyone's home. So who opens the door to let this stuff in, and how does it get past the pastoral and elder leadership? Their books, worship lyrics, CDs, DVDs, seminars, podcasts, websites, and concerts use terms, quotes, images, and concepts that appear on the surface to be mainline "Christian". It appears to be all about heaven, the Spirit, the Presence, and deeper 24/7 prayer - not the typical "red flags" that alert people to cults. This chapter identifies the six doors by which the NAR's *entertaining deception* enters into a Calvary Chapel.

Door Number-1: Worship

Jamie Brown's insightful article: "Is Evangelical Worship Headed For A Huge Crash?" (HealthyLeaders.com - 10/21/2016) focused on what is perhaps the primary doorway. The time in worship during any church service — whether in a large sanctuary-auditorium, a smaller fellowship hall, an outreach concert, or someone's home for a Bible study - worship lyrics provide a wide open door for introducing false ideas about God, heaven, the Holy Spirit, healing, miracles, and Jesus. There are many readily recognizable songs sung during Calvary Chapel worship that have very catchy melodies, easy to sing and remember, and gets a lot of regular play-time in the car, at home, or at work through the radio, CDs, iPod, smartphone, Spotify, or Pandora. And the lyrics are about: "Jesus", "Presence", "glory", and "yearning" so it must be okay, right?

A major "new" movement in NAR church worship accepts artistic license as equal to, or more important than, sound doctrine. This has enabled many musicians and worship leaders to author a "new" generation of lyrics that are less and less about praising to the Lord, while being more and more about personal thoughts, experiences, and interpretations of the songwriter. Many songs are now about people singing their needs, desires, and yearnings, pleading about our hurting, pain, and feelings of being far from God. Others focus on singing about ourselves, who we are, and our value to Him. Popular lyrics use allegorical images with no Biblical basis to envision and symbolize God. One "new" worship genre has been nicknamed "Jesus as my boyfriend", where lyrics cross the line into various romantic images and comments that sound like a dating relationship love song. These introduce deceptive themes as if they are sound Biblical truths. Consider these examples:

"Kisses from heaven of joy and laughter, I want to lavish my love on you Jesus"

[God] "is the air that I breathe, I'm desperate for you"

"We're heaven spun creations, His pride and adoration, safe within His promise of calling and of destiny"

"We're going to dance on the river, we're stirring up deep, deep wells"
"I wanna sit at your feet, drink from the cup of your hand, lay back against you and breathe, hear your heartbeat . . . it's more than I can stand"

"I'm caught up in the passion of an ever-flaming fire . . . we're lovesick"

"Won't you dance with me, O lover of my soul?"

"I'm drowning in your sea of forgetfulness, my chains of yesterday surround me I'm just one mistake away from you leaving me this way"

"When the stars came crashing down in tiny pieces to the ground, I spun around and caught a flame [and] gave into a God I didn't know"

Many popular NAR worship images depict God's Spirit as some kind of force, or energy, or meandering wind that has to be beckoned by the worship leader and invited to come and join the congregation. It's all about waiting for, looking for, anticipating the "presence" to finally arrive, then He can fill the physical location (refer to Chapter-4 and the Tabernacle of David). But the Bible teaches He already dwells in the hearts of all believers [1st Corinthians 6:13 *Do you not*

know that you are a temple of God and the Spirit of God dwells in you? ; and verse-19 *Do you not know that your body is a temple of the Holy Spirit who is in you, whom you have from God, and that you are not your own?"* This is confirmed in 2nd Timothy 1:14 *"the Holy Spirit who dwells in you",* Romans 8:11 *"the Spirit of Him who raised Jesus from the dead dwells in you",* Galatians 4:6 *"God has sent the Spirit of His Son into our hearts",* and God states very plainly that He *"does not dwell in houses made by human hands"* [Acts 7:48]. Why then does the Spirit have to be invited to come to the worship service, as with these two popular worship songs?

> *"Holy Spirit you are welcome here come flood this place and fill the atmosphere to be OVERCOME by your presence Lord"*

> *"Blow through the CAVERNS of my soul, Spirit come and fill this place, let your glory now INVADE"*

The BabylonBee.com lampoons this deceptive flaw of contemporary NAR worship with the following satire (as if reported from a recent worship service), *"the third Person of the Trinity patiently waited in the foyer through several songs Sunday morning, before finally entering the main sanctuary to flood the place and fill the atmosphere".* But how sad it is that this is exactly what's being sung at many Calvary Chapels, and is often the opening prayer of worship leaders preparing the congregation to wait for/long for the "presence".

Worship leaders have also begun to preface the time in music with introductory remarks like, "Oh Lord, we're here this morning because we're hurting, we're full of doubts, and we're desperate for your touch in our lives, so let your fire fall on us and overwhelm us" - or "Father, we're here this evening because we're broken, we're searching, we're empty, and we're fearful, so we need heaven to come down right now, show us your glory, let us tremble before you, consume us all now, and fill this place with your presence". [Both of these introductions are word-for-word transcripts from multiple recordings I've made at a wide range of Calvary Chapel worship services.] Again, how sad that the theme for worship would be about us having hurt, doubts, and fears - when the introduction to worship should be more like, "Lord, we are here to honor you, to lift your name on high, to worship you and give you all the glory due your name, so as we turn our attention to you, speak to our hearts and prepare us to hear from your Word, and we pray this in Jesus name, Amen".

It's The End Of The Worship As We Know It

You might remember REM's Michael Stipe singing face-paced lyrics that bemoaned a perceived breakdown of various societal institutions and norms as he summed it all up with "It's the end of the world as we know it". This could serve as a pop-culture metaphor for the contemporary church regarding the gradual dismantling of congregational worship, as NAR deception and its musician-messengers are re-defining, re-positioning, and re-packaging church worship into a multimedia event focused on things other than the Lord. Many of my "live" visits to NAR worship services, combined with watching dozens of online videos of these prophets, apostles, and musicians, have led me to define this current crisis as "It's the end of the *worship* as we know it" — because the changes are THAT dramatic. I had a 1-on-1 discussion with a heavily NAR-influenced Calvary Chapel worship leader to discuss this troubling new direction in which he is leading at his church. His apathetic lack of concern and complete inability to recognize any of the key Biblical doctrines I raised were a very sad commentary on his lack of concern and spiritual discernment. That fit well with the trailing lyrics in that iconic REM song title: (". . . and I feel fine"). He listened to my comments, wrote down some notes, but in the end stated very clearly that "thanks for your concerns, but I think I'm good".

Thom Schultz wrote an excellent editorial article "Why They Don't Sing On Sunday Anymore" (HealthyLeaders.com - 02/16/2017) noting the current trend of church worship moving further and further into being an entertaining concert that the congregation watches and listens to, instead of being pastoral servants who truly lead the church body into a time of corporate worship. In fact many churches now have an "Artistic Director" responsible for the media-staging of props, flat-screens, and overall presentation of the worship service.

Bethel Leads Calvary?

Many Calvary Chapel worship leaders have fully embraced NAR worship music styles, lyrics, and stage practices as the contemporary standards for how worship happens, and what to sing in their own church services. I have first-hand knowledge of a Calvary Chapel in southern California whose worship leader took his entire team of musicians to the Bethel Music Jesus Culture night of worship hosted by Mariner's Church in Irvine, CA. This particular worship leader has already introduced NAR-influenced music and lyrics at his church, and the Bethel worship conference further enforced this among all the musicians on his worship team. What was even more troubling was to learn that they all attended this event without any knowledge of the senior pastor, assistant pastors, or elders - demonstrating a complete lack of spiritual oversight and accountability from that Calvary Chapel' leadership.

The Litmus Test

As a lifelong musician and worship leader, having played in numerous outreach bands, and spent hundreds of hours in sound studios recording original music, I definitely understand how a catchy melody with great vocal and instrumentation arrangements can readily become a favorite song for a church congregation. But let's never forget the LYRICS that are sung to God in worship and praise to Him. The typical church attendee probably expects the pastor to take great care in his sermon preparation, but is there a similar focus on doctrinal truth in the preparation of the content in the worship lyrics? The best way to evaluate what the church is *entertaining* in its worship is to simply review each song's lyrics in paragraph form, as if they were a pastor's study notes for a sermon. Then just read through and compare these to sound doctrine from God's Word. Do this separate from that catchy melody and powerful crescendo on the final chorus. Can the lyrics stand firmly on their own? For example, read through this worship song (without the melody) and ask yourself, "Is this what I would want preached by a pastor on a Sunday morning?"

> *He is jealous for me and loves like a hurricane and I am a tree bending beneath the weight of His wind and mercy. When all of a sudden I am unaware of these afflictions eclipsed by glory and I realize just how beautiful you are and how great your affections are for me. And oh how He loves us. We are His portion and He is our prize, drawn to redemption by the grace in his eyes. If grace is an ocean we're all sinking. Heaven meets earth like a sloppy wet kiss and my heart turns violently inside of my chest, and I don't have time to maintain these regrets when I think about the way He loves us.* – David Crowder

The is essentially nothing in the content of this verbiage that is consistent with sound doctrine from God's Word. Instead, it's just a rambling series of poetic-allegorical images from someone's personal ideas and perspectives about God - all protected under the relative safety of "artistic license". For the highly impressionable, spiritually immature, and undiscerning in the congregation, these lyrics will develop in them ideas and thoughts about our Lord that are entirely unbiblical. The very real questions a person would have in response to this include: He loves me like a HURRICANE? I am a TREE that bends under His WIND? His MERCY is pressing down heavy on me? All of a sudden I am unaware of WHAT afflictions? That are eclipsed by glory? I am God's PORTION? He is my PRIZE? So, grace is like an OCEAN and we're all DROWNING in it? How does heaven meet earth with a SLOPPY WET KISS? My heart should turn VIOLENTLY inside my chest? What are the REGRETS I don't have time to maintain? If this was a pastor's sermon, he would earn a failing grade for preparation, theology, and ability to articulate God's Word. Now let's apply the same Litmus Test to this popular worship song:

> *My Jesus my Savior, Lord there is none like You. All of my days I want to praise the wonders of Your mighty love. My comfort, my shelter, a tower of refuge and strength, let every breath, all that I am never cease to worship You. Shout to the Lord all the earth let us sing power and majesty praise to the King. The mountains bow down and the seas will roar at the sound of Your name. I sing for joy at the works of Your hand, forever I'll love You forever I'll stand. Nothing compares to the promise I have in You.* — Chris Tomlin

Where's the focus? On the Lord. What's the content? Sound doctrine from clear Biblical truths about the Lord's eternal nature and His attributes. Enough said.

Another very disconcerting example is the worship song Forever written by female pastor Kari Jobe at deceptive NAR Gateway Church in Southlake, Texas. Her artistic license skips right past sound doctrine and supports the same false teaching promoted by NAR apostles Kenneth Copeland, Joyce Meyer, Mike Bickel, Bill Johnson, and others that Jesus died a "spiritual death" and was the very first person ever "born-again". In her own words on a YouTube video interview she states clearly that her song is about *"that time in between [after Jesus died on the cross] when Jesus was in hell rendering hell and ransacking hell and defeating the enemy"*. Use the Litmus Test on Jobe's lyrics:

> *One final breath He gave as heaven looked away*
> *The Son of God was laid in darkness, a battle in the grave*
> *The war on death was waged, the power of hell forever broken*

These lyrics provide sensational imagery, but also some very bad and deceptive doctrine, because Jesus declared victory over death when he breathed his last on the cross. And while He did deliver Old Testament believers captive from Sheol, Jesus was not doing battle in hell to finish His work, because He already proclaimed "it is finished" from the cross. The Greek word in the perfect tense, τελέω [teleo] means "is accomplished", and the term Tetelestai means "it is finished" used in John 19:28 and 30. Once again, a popular worship melody is *entertaining deception* with a false narrative about the events of Jesus' death.

Because the NAR holds to replacement theology (see Chapter-5), many of their worship songs include lyrics from the Old Testament that are speaking specifically about the literal nation of Israel, which are then misapplied and to the contemporary church. For example, there are numerous worship songs about the "dry bones coming back to life", applying Ezekiel 37 prophecy about Israel back in the land instead to believers today, as God puts us back together. Similar misappropriations include singing like we're Israel in the wilderness, as per Matt Redman's lyrics about waiting for the cloud by day, the pillar of fire by night, the priests trembling, the fire falling "and then Your glory came".

Door Number-2: Prayer

The NAR has completely re-written the role of prayer, from the simple and pure communion a person can have anytime, anywhere with the Lord - to special WAYS to pray, how to PREPARE for "better" prayer, and those SECRETS to unlock the power of prayer. Add in visualization, contemplation, and trance-mantra-like repetition (see Chapter-4), and these "new" ways to pray are an easy doorway into Calvary Chapel. This *Entertaining deception* can easily slide in when just one person checks out "Contemplative Prayer" at a website and begins to try it out personally at home. He then delves a little deeper into related online searches and finds information about "Sozo Prayer" or "Lectio Divina" and decides to give these a try as well. The next step is to introduce these in men's discipleship or at a home group. But Jesus instructs us to NOT do all the rituals, special postures, and chanting like the religious leaders who want the attention of men [Matthew 6:5-6]. Instead Jesus said to simply, quietly, without any fanfare go individually, personally, privately before the Lord where no one sees (except the Lord) and speak to Him directly.

Door Number-3: Books

False teachings of the NAR can also get into Calvary Chapels through books — some even sold at Calvary bookstores. In the first type, the titles are forthright about their deceptive NAR content. In the second type, the titles are not as explicit, but might not sound quite right. The third type are titles that read like mainstream topics, and are so subtle in their NAR allusions that they easily draw in the unsuspecting person who is unaware of the NAR authorship or publishing house. Here are some examples of the explicit first type:

- *SOZO Saved Healed Delivered* (2016) by Teresa Liebscher, Dawna DeSilva, and Danny Silk

- *Prayers That Rout Demons* (2014) by John Eckhardt

- *Church Quake! The Explosive Power Of The New Apostolic Reformation* (1999) by C. Peter Wagner

- *Financial SOZO* (2011) by Stephen DeSilva

- *The Apostolic Ministry* (2004) by Rick Joyner

- *Wrestling With Dark Angels* (1990) by C. Peter Wagner

- *You Need More Money* (2000) by Brian Houston

- *Step Into Supernatural Provision: Keys To Living In Financial Abundance* (2015) by Patricia King

- *Money And The Prosperous Soul* (2016) by Stephen DeSilva

- *Basics Of Dreams, Visions, And Strange Events* (2004) by John Paul Jackson

- *Kundalini Energy And Christian Spirituality* (2016) by Philip St. Romain

- *Manifesting Your Spirit* (2010) by Graham Cooke

The second type of titles are not as up-front about their false NAR topics, but their *entertaining deception* becomes apparent to the discerning heart once the Table of Contents and first few chapter is read. It's so sad that these books have all been unwittingly read by people who attend Calvary Chapels, who thought them to be helpful, encouraging, and even inspiring:

- *Unlocking Heaven's Power* (2015) by John Paul Jackson

- *Growing In The Prophetic* (1995) by Mike Bickel

- *Walking In The Supernatural: Another Cup Of Spiritual Java* (2003) by Beni Johnson

- *Army Of The Dawn* (2015) by Rick Joyner

- *The Great Procession: From The Castle Of Religion To The Forest Of God's Kingdom* (2014) by Jacob Reeve

- *Power Thoughts* (2010) by Joyce Meyer

- *Invading Babylon: The 7 Mountain Mandate* (2013) by Lance Wallnau and Bill Johnson

- *Developing A Supernatural Lifestyle: Practical Guide To A Life Of Signs, Wonders, Miracles* (2003) by Kris Vallotton

- *Unmasking The Jezebel Spirit* (2001) by John Paul Jackson

- *Birthing The Miraculous* (2014) by Heidi Baker

- *Call Me Crazy But I'm Hearing God's Voice: Secrets To Hearing God's Voice* (2007) Kim Clement

- *Developing Your Prophetic Gifts* (2003) John Paul Jackson

- *Developing Your Prophetic Gifting* (1994) Graham Cooke

The third type has a title that at face value seems mainline "Christian". But these are the most deceptive, as many people at Calvary Chapels - even pastors, elders, and other leaders - have these on their personal bookshelves and consult them for women's fellowships, married couples, or men's groups.

The following titles have been embraced by many well-meaning Christians, and some are even sold in the bookstores at Calvary Chapel churches:

- *Jesus Calling* (2004) by Sarah Young

- *The Call* (2006) by Rick Joyner

- *You Can Have A New Beginning* (20109) by Morris Cerullo

- *In The Zone: Living A Life In God's Blessing* (2003) by Patricia King

- *You Can, You Will* (2014) by Joel Osteen

- *Beautiful One: A Walk In Deeper Intimacy With The One Who Created Us* (2010) by Beni Johnson

- *School Of Jesus Identity Foundations* (2003) Jacob Reeve

- *Trusting God Day By Day* (2012) by Joyce Meyer

- *The Jesus Fast: The Call To Awaken The Nations* (2016) by Lou Engle

- *The Purpose Driven Life* (2016) by Rick Warren

Rick Warren's book is in the offices of many pastors, elders, staff, and lay leaders throughout Calvary Chapels (over 30 million sold worldwide). But just this one comment from the author should be enough to give everyone serious concern about the NAR message of this book, *"Personal computers have brand names, but inside every PC is an Intel chip and an operating system, Windows;*

The Purpose Driven paradigm is the Intel chip - the Windows system of the 21st century church" (Christianity Today, October-2005). He also disregards any challenge to his purpose-driven teachings with: *"Be willing to let people leave the church; people are going to leave no matter what you do; but when you define the vision, you're choosing who leaves. [If] you say, 'But Rick, they're the pillars of the church' now you know what pillars [really] are - pillars are people who hold things up. In your church, you may have to have some blessed subtractions before you have any real additions"* (Rick Warren speaking at: 'Building A Purpose-Driven Church", January - 1998 at Saddleback Church).

Door Number-4: Events

Many of the undiscerning and unaware at Calvary Chapel churches play an interesting game of "shuffle" in how they seek a closer walk with God. They go to a Sunday morning service at Calvary, maybe even a midweek service or Bible study; but they also regularly show up at all kinds of NAR false doctrine conferences, seminars, concerts, workshops, and special events. But you can't have one foot in each. The sound doctrine from Calvary will be in direct conflict with the mixed messages of kingdom-now dominionism, latter rain, and bridal eschatology. And how can slain in the spirit, Sozo prayer, toking the ghost, and gold dust glory clouds fit with the services and ministries at Calvary? The reality is that many people at Calvary are spiritually undiscerning and don't understand any differences with a "Night of Prophecy", "Let The Fire Fall" rally, "Bethel Music Worship Night", or "Unlocking Your Prophetic" seminar.

Door Number-5: Web Content

Many at Calvary will also be introduced to NAR false teachings through the web - watching YouTube videos and podcasts, downloading MP3 teachings, getting a daily prophecy word email to their inbox, and reading all the articles, PDFs, and personal testimonies about signs, wonders, miracles, healings, and wild predictions by Apostles. We all know there's no filter on web content, as anyone can post whatever they want, with little or no discernment. This instant accessibility is very problematic because literally "anything goes" (and does).

Door Number-6: Personal Relationships

The final door is lunch with a co-worker, talking with a friend on the phone, coffee with a neighbor, or forwarding web links and posts from Facebook to family members. People get introduced to ALL kinds of unfiltered deception from their personal relationships. It's an easy offer in a casual friendly setting, and in no time, the false teachings have spread among dozens, hundreds, even thousands across various networks. Thankfully, God's Word can always be that trusted plumb line or level that checks these personal referrals for Biblical accuracy. The next chapter examines a large sample of who's who across many sectors of the contemporary NAR.

CHAPTER SEVEN
Who's Who In Today's NAR

Apostles, Prophets, Churches, Ministries

Chapter-4 introduced a wide range of signs, wonders, and miracles that are the focus of the modern day NAR. This chapter is designed to be a ready-reference guide about these NAR Apostles and Prophets, as well as their Churches, Schools, and Ministries found all across the U.S. and in dozens of foreign countries. A quick reminder that the book by Doug Gievett and Holly Pivec, *A New Apostolic Reformation? A Biblical Response To A Worldwide Movement* is a great resource to get more details on all things in the NAR.

Here in this chapter, I want to provide those in Calvary Chapel with a list of the people and places I have personally researched and encountered first-hand who are having influence and impact on church life in Calvary Chapels. My strongest admonition is that if any of these names show up in a pastors-elders meeting, or in discussions about a book, magazine, video, DVD, podcast, music CD or MP3 download — or website, conference, workshop, concert, or other special event related to people in your Calvary Chapel church, be very quick to recognize it as *entertaining deception*. Call it out for others in your ministry area, bring it to the pastors and elders, and take a strong stand against allowing it any kind of foothold where it could begin to spread false doctrine.

This list is of course not exhaustive, as there are literally hundreds of modern day NAR Apostles, Prophets, Healers, and their related organizations in the U.S. and worldwide. What was once thought of as a fringe movement, the NAR is now firmly entrenched on the contemporary "Christian" landscape, and has a more mainline reputation and brand in American churches for its claims that the Third Wave of God's Spirit is in full force, so you better not miss this "New" work, built on "Apostolic" leaders, in a watershed "Reformation" of the global Christian church. In each case I provide my notes, links, and citations.

C. Peter Wagner, Fuller Seminary

He coined the term "New Apostolic Reformation" and declared it to be the "Third Wave" through his more than three-dozen books published since the 1980s. He died in October 2016 and was eulogized by the NAR-Pentecostal community as "Truly One Of God's Generals" *Charisma News,* October 24, 2016. He was self-declared as "the presiding Apostle" over more than 200 men and women listed on the International Coalition of Apostles, and also said that ALL churches must ultimately come under his (ICA) apostolic authority as "God is shifting and establishing His [new] church government foundation".

John Wimber, Vineyard

He is right behind Wagner in his influence ushering in the NAR through his writings and teachings in the Vineyard Christian Fellowship movement that now numbers some 2,300 individual churches worldwide. He died in 1997.

Rick Joyner, Morningstar

His MorningstarMinistries.org is popular in the NAR, including schools, churches, publications, ministries, missions, and MornigstarTV.com to promote his false teachings and deceptive doctrines. He is known for stating "Jesus is not a man, He was and is a Spirit", while his book *Final Quest* is his prophetic word that the war to bring Jesus' return and kingdom is already underway.

Bill & Beni Johnson, Bethel Church

Two very popular NAR Apostles-Prophets, they oversee a large ministry campus in Redding, CA that includes a church, music studios, publishing house, and the Bethel School of Supernatural Ministry. Their message is typical Word-of-Faith false doctrine and Kingdom Now Dominionism, signs and wonders, and their church originated the gold dust glory cloud, angel feathers, and jewels in worship services. They openly support the "Kansas City Prophets" [see: Bickle, Cain, Jones, Jackson, Engle], and prosperity doctrine Apostle Benny Hinn. Bill has infamously said, "God is in charge but not in control; He has left us in control". He also teaches Jesus was no longer God when He was on the cross.

Jesus Culture - Bethel Music

The worship-music band at Bethel Church, Jesus Culture [JC] supports Bill and Beni Johnson's false teachings with worship lyrics focused on NAR dominionism, latter rain signs and wonders, and convincing young people they are the Manifest Sons of God - Joel's Army. JC music is the set-up for Holy Spirit Fire Tunnels (see online videos) and recruiting young men and women to serve at Bethel, or enroll in the Bethel School of Supernatural Ministry. Bethel Music lyrics teach-promote unbiblical concepts about God, the Holy Spirit, and Jesus with phrases such as: "Like a tidal wave crashing over me Your love is fierce".

Kris Vallotton

Also based at Bethel Church in Redding alongside the Johnsons, he is the author of some two-dozen NAR-themed books on signs, wonders, and supernatural miracles. He infamously said this about Bethel, *"A small, yet influential coalition of people has shared negative reports about us [using the] words 'controversial', 'unbalanced' or even 'cult'. I can understand why certain religious leaders view us through these perspectives; we certainly have made our share of mistakes, both as a leadership team and those who follow us. We have a research and development culture where people are encouraged to take risks. We view ourselves as pioneers [rather] than settlers, therefore, we celebrate creativity, revelation, invention above comfort, safety and security".*

Bethel School of Supernatural Ministry

The flagship educational and training entity of the Bethel brand, it has on average around 1,000 people taking classes that teach how to do miracles, speak prophecy, heal, and do fantastic signs and wonders. The website often notes that the upcoming term's course offerings "are subject to the leading of the Holy Spirit and can change at any time". Many people from Calvary Chapel here in Santa Barbara - and ten other area Calvary churches - have enrolled in BSSM online courses, and several have done their studies up at that northern California campus. Graduates tell about world-reaching prophecies spoken over them during their time in Redding, a few are now recognized as an "Apostle" or "Prophet", and minister at local Houses of Prayer (IHOP) and healing rooms.

Lance Wallnau

A self-proclaimed disciple of C. Peter Wagner, he teaches false doctrine through his books *Invading Babylon* (2013, co-author Bill Johnson), and *The 7-Mountain Mandate* (2009) - repackaging dominionism and bridal eschatology into a message of end-times hope for people to usher in God's Kingdom. He speaks at men's groups, retreats, and conferences, with a focus on locating and mentoring those with senior management positions to influence the taking of those 7 mountains — contrary to Jesus' teaching [Matthew 24] that the end-times would be about false teachers and God's judgment of sin on the earth.

Brian & Bobbie Houston, Hillsong

This husband and wife co-pastors of Hillsong Church (founded by Brian's father), they oversee Hillsong Music. Their emergent-church message tells people to simply "believe and you will be changed". Their seeker-friendly prosperity doctrine is covered in Brian's 1999 book *You Need More Money*. Hillsong is part of the Australian Christian Churches of the Assemblies of God, and firmly supports the Latter Rain and Kingdom Now Dominionism teachings of dreams, hopes, and aspirations to bring God's kingdom to earth. The Hillsong church and conferences drive traffic to Hillsong concerts, CDs, and movies ("Let Hope Rise"), drive traffic to Hillsong Leadership College, and so on, and so on.

Hillsong Music

This Christian music label is arguably the most popular brand of worship music worldwide. But the message on their 60 albums and at huge worship conferences (attended by tens of thousands) does not present the true gospel of Jesus Christ's death at Calvary and our need to repent of sin and be forgiven. Instead, their "close-to-Christian" lyrics include: "Spirit lead me where my trust is without borders", "With fire in our eyes our lives alight Your love untamed", "You didn't want heaven without us so You brought heaven down", and of course, "there is a love that never holds you back so won't you break free?"

Lou Engle, The Call

His ministry campus is located in Colorado Springs and he puts on dozens of conferences each year. His itinerant mega-revival event "Azusa Now: The Call" is fixated on reproducing the 1906 supposed wild signs, wonders, and miracles that occurred on Azusa Street in Los Angeles - hailed as the catalyst of the modern Pentecostal movement. He kissed the feet of a high ranking Catholic official to symbolize reconciliation between Catholics and Protestants, agreeing that the doctrinal divisions between the two is a "diabolical sin" and "Jesus doesn't care that Catholics and Protestants disagree on Bible doctrine".

Mike Bickle, International House of Prayer

He launched the infamous "Kansas City Prophets" movement of the late 1980s that told every pastor at all the churches in the greater Kansas City area that they needed to merge their churches into Mike's new Metro Christian Fellowship - the only "one true church", which became the International House of Prayer (IHOP). The HOP model spread all around the country setting up 24/7 prayer rooms and healing rooms, as well as prophesying over and anointing dozens of new Apostles. IHOP-Kansas City has become a destination hub for many Calvary Chapel youth desiring to be called out by the Holy Spirit as that special end-times generation (Joel's Army) of super-elite Christians whose worship, dreams, prophecies, and signs will hasten Christ's return.

House of Prayer in/near Your City

Check out the IHOP website directory to find the House of Prayer and/or Healing Room near your Calvary Chapel, as this is one of the most common entrees for people into the false teachings of the NAR. Once the spiritually immature and undiscerning have been prayed and prophesied over with amazing words like "you will change the world and impact millions for the coming Kingdom", or told they possess latent, untapped supernatural spiritual gifts, watch out! This begins the "one foot in Calvary, one foot in IHOP" that introduces spiritual deception within Calvary Chapel (see more in Chapter-6).

IHOP University

Similar to Bethel's school, this "university" has now become a ministry destination for many college graduates from here in Santa Barbara, in addition to attracting thousands more from all over the world to come and be trained in signs, wonders, miracles, healing, and prophecy. Afterward, many get ministry positions at an IHOP or other NAR-friendly church. One listed his job position title on the local HOP web page as "Anointed Facilitator Of Bliss".

Bob Jones, Kansas City Prophet

Not the founder of the university in Greenville, South Carolina, THIS Bob Jones was the prophet who spoke words over Mike Bickle in 1983 that resulted in Bickle launching what later became the International House of Prayer. Jones made hundreds of wild predictions about the church, the end times, and the Latter Rain, Kingdom-Now Dominionism that laid the foundation for the rise of the NAR through the various Kansas City Prophets. He infamously claimed that Acts 2:42 *"and they were continuously devoting themselves to the Apostles' teachings"* was specifically speaking about him! He died in 2014.

Paul Cain, Santa Maria Healing Rooms

One of the original Kansas City Prophets alongside Bob Jones and Mike Bickle, he is now located just an hour up the 101 freeway from Santa Barbara and oversees the IHOP Healing Rooms Apostolic Center in Santa Maria, CA while he (according to his website) continues to receive daily revelations from heaven and is "about to release the word of the Lord over nations and to the church". He claims that at age 19 he was visited by an angel in warrior clothing pointing to a billboard stating :Joel's Army In Training". *Charisma* magazine reported in 2005 he was removed from spiritual fellowship by three church leaders for his habitual pattern of unbiblical behavior, including alcoholism and homosexuality.

Patricia King, Extreme Prophetic

She is one of the most popular female NAR Apostles and a Prophetess who has written dozens of books focused on Kingdom Now Dominion (her book *The Bride Makes Herself Ready*) and self-improvement themes of ascending to a higher God consciousness (her book *Step Into Supernatural Provision*). In perhaps her most infamous Apostolic vision-revelations she claims she has been to heaven and seen barrel after barrel in the Lord's wine cellar, telling her audience they can get drunk the right way, God's way, as she declares "so come on, in Jesus name, the bar is open and drink, drink, drink, drink".

John Paul Jackson, Stream Ministries

Another of the Kansas City Prophets, he served with John Wimber at the Anaheim Vineyard, then with Mike Bickle's KC-Metro church, before launching Streams Ministries that focused on miraculous prophecies and his own form of Gnosticism (having special, secret, inner knowledge) showcased in wild prophecies and his proprietary (unbiblical) system for interpreting dreams and visions. He infamously prophesied in 2009 about "the perfect storm" coming in 2010 and the "woes of 2012" – none of which ever came to pass. His 2006 book *7 Days Behind The Veil* boasted of his personal trip to heaven and what it's like in heaven's throne room, touching what you've only dreamed about- discovering your dreams were far too small. He died in 2015.

Streams Institute for Spiritual Development

Jackson's self-directed school through which over 12,000 people took his courses, and bought his books, CDs, DVDs, and self-study workbooks for classes such as: *The Art of Hearing God, Understanding Dreams And Visions, Advanced Workshop In Dreams And Visions,* and *Limitless: How To Release*

Creative Intelligence (wasn't that the 2011 Bradley Cooper movie?) These online programs are as popular as ever, with his faithful followers continuing to lead courses, seminars, and workshops all over the world.

John & Carol Arnott, Catch The Fire

These husband-wife co-pastors were the leaders of the Toronto Airport Vineyard, infamous for the holy laughter and barking phenomena in the 1990s. Now renamed Catch The Fire, they continue to teach and write about signs and wonders, and are known [by *Charisma News*] as two of the most anointed "Holy Ghost bartenders". Their website describes how "desperately dry Christians fly into Toronto from all over the world to get refilled on their "new wine". Enough said, due to their clear lack of Biblical understanding about the Holy Spirit.

Graham Cooke, Brilliant Perspectives

He is an itinerant NAR Prophet who speaks at conferences and men's groups about his book *Developing Your Prophetic Gifting* , but teaches the false doctrine that God's judgment concluded at the cross, so there's no additional judgment until the Great White Throne in Revelation 20:11-15. He tries to be like Tony Robbins with positive-thinking New-Age self-betterment, but through prophesy. At the 2009 "Voice of the Prophets" his "Decree" said God is about favor and vengeance "INSTEAD"; "it's time to turn the table on your enemies, heaven has come down INSTEAD of hell, Jesus has come INSTEAD of the devil -

live the life you've always wanted INSTEAD of the life you've always had". He's spoken here in Santa Barbara a few times, with his typical a signs and wonders miracle prophecy message, but always with very bad doctrine and theology.

Chuck Pierce, Glory of Zion

He likes to re-interpret Bible prophecy about Israel with his replacement theology, always claiming the "dry bones" in Ezekiel 37 are today's Christians, spiritually parched and lifeless, being supernaturally raised to life. That Biblical image is clearly spoken to Israel - fulfilled in 1948 as the nation is reassembled after 2,000 years. He co-opts other passages about Israel, like "bestowing a mantle" on people [like Elijah to Elisha in 1st Kings 19]. In 2000 he confessed (along with NAR prophetess Cindy Jacobs) in *National School of The Prophets* about the systemic inaccuracy of his prophecies not coming to pass, "I've made a lot of mistakes, there's no excuse, I need to do better, and ask forgiveness for my immaturity and inaccuracy of my office". Once again, enough said.

Cindy Jacobs

She is considered the spiritual "mother" (overseer) of the Jesus Culture band at Bethel Church, speaking dozens of prophetic words about their music and its impact on "bringing the Kingdom to earth". She regularly posts "new" prophecies about terrorist attacks in the U.S. [2014], and always has her "out" - that if anything close to it happens, then she was correct; but if nothing close occurs, she claims that "not enough people were praying alongside her word". Her prophecies typically have broad 2-3 year windows of time to occur, and are vague enough to allow for multiple events to be attributed to that prediction.

Morris Cerrullo, MC World Evangelism

He is perhaps the co-leader (alongside Joel Osteen) in the word-of-faith and prosperity doctrine movement, and claims that at age 14 two angels led him to heaven from his orphanage to speak with God [see his *Miracle Book*] who told him he would prophesy the future. He refers to himself as "Dr. Cerrullo" but has no such earned degree, and infamously claims that "God's plan from the beginning of time was always to reproduce Himself". He says he heals people, has sold anointed 'Holy Ghost handkerchiefs" [trying to replicate Acts 19:12], but all his word-of-faith and healing miracles remain unverified.

Todd Bentley, Fresh Fire

This false prophet offers online courses: "Living In The Supernatural", and "Dreams-Visions-Signs-and-Wonders" and his "Secret Place" conferences. He was anointed by NAR Apostles after his 2008 revival rallies in Lakeland, FL drew thousands and he supposedly raised people from the dead. His moves of the Holy Spirit include violent breaking of tables and doors, and says he was once possessed by 25 demons. The most troubling video of him is standing alongside a woman supposedly spirit-filled and speaking a prophecy in tongues.

[the Bible teaches tongues are praise TO God, not words FROM God] as she violently shakes her head and screams unintelligibly, while Todd yells in the microphone "C'mon Jesus, let's see more of you". Enough said - false Apostle!

LaVerne Adams, "Doctor of Destiny"

A certified life coach/motivational speaker, she is the female version of Rick Warren, who did the Foreword for her book *Driven By Destiny: 12 Secrets To Unlock Your Future* (red flags of "secrets" "destiny" "unlock"). She attracts thousands to her website, conferences, seminars, podcasts, and books. She proclaims in her book: "I decree that transformation is taking place - everything in the universe must line up to make it happen because IT'S MY DESTINY, and I am settling for nothing less". She's simply a New Age guru-wanna-be like John Bradshaw, merging psycho-babble with a few Biblical phrases and images.

Rodney & Adonica Howard-Browne, Revival Ministries

This South African couple also co-pastor The River (church) in Tampa, was one of the originators of the Toronto Blessing (holy laughter), and being "God's Bartender" to get people drunk in the spirit, while falling uncontrollably "under the power" - believing he is God's vessel to distribute the spirit globally.

Che & Sue Ahn, Harvest International

This husband-wife team started Hrock church in Pasadena - and now lead *Harvest International* (yet another ministry with the same brand name of

Greg Laurie's church and outreaches). Another NAR Apostle closely affiliated with Bethel's Bill Johnson, as well as John Arnott and Todd Bentley.

Byron Easterling, Night of Prophecy

He is an itinerant Apostle-Prophet who travels from city to city doing his special brand of NAR prophecy nights, always telling the audience "God loves to send love notes to His kids and I'm so glad I get to be the translator of His heart for our time together". His standard program starts with his "prophetic word" that this particular city has high walls all around it with dark spiritual forces keeping out the presence, the glory, the work of God. Then the rest of the service is all kinds of signs, wonders, words of knowledge, lots of prophecy against the darkness, and of course concludes with Byron telling the audience he sees the walls crumbling, the high places coming down, with the demons in full retreat and the city now ready for "heaven to invade" (Bill Johnson's book).

Heidi & Rolland Baker, Iris Global

She has branded herself as a global missionary emphasizing signs, wonders, and her trademark outreach "birthing the miraculous". Her videos always focus on amazing tales from her travels in Africa where she claims to have raised the dead dozens of times and healed hundreds of people. She is a co-author of *The Reformer's Pledge*, along with C. Peter Wagner, Bill Johnson, Lance Wallnau, Chuck Pierce, Lou Engle, and the Arnotts. Her videos show her laying hands on people as she "imparts the presence" while they scream, roll around, shake - and she proclaims, "I think he's got it" ("it" is the Holy Spirit).

Brian Simmons, The Passion

This NAR 'wish-I-was-a-Bible scholar' authored his own Bible translation (The Passion), telling Sid Roth, host of the show "It's Supernatural" that in 2009 Jesus Christ appeared and breathed on him the "spirit of special revelation", telling him to write this "new" Bible. He infamously claims he went to heaven during a dream and "shoplifted" from heaven's library a 22nd chapter of the Gospel of John (there are 21 chapters of John in the Bible). This "new" chapter describes a "greater works generation" not seen in the original version who will do ALL the same miracles of Jesus to bring about the Kingdom. How convenient is that? - to pen your own additional content to fit NAR doctrine.

Summary

Whenever any of these individuals, churches, schools, or ministries comes up in conversation, or are mentioned with regard to a book, website, or special event, be on the alert. Compare what they say, do, and sing to God's Word and be prepared to take a stand against their false teachings. The next chapter describes how each of the Calvary Chapel distinctives outlined by Pastor Chuck is directly challenged by the deceptions from the NAR.

CHAPTER EIGHT
Challenging Calvary Distinctives

Remember This Foundation

Pastor Chuck penned a very important book, *Calvary Chapel Distinctives* (The Word For Today, 2000) to clearly outline 13 core facets that have defined the Calvary Chapel movement since the 1970s. These have always been the hallmarks of the great consistency throughout the 1,700 churches around the world. However, he was quick to point out in his opening Preface "this is not to say that all Calvary Chapels are identical [as] I am always amazed at how God can take simple, basic elements and create such variety out of them". But the key point was that those "simple, basic elements" were consistently the same, regardless of the location of the Calvary Chapel. This chapter looks at each of the twelve distinctives and the specific challenge to each coming from NAR deception and false teachings. It's time for Calvary pastors, elders, deacons, lay leaders, and all who attend to stand firm on sound Biblical doctrine, and "always be ready to provide a clear defense to everyone who would ask for an account of the hope that is in you" [1st Peter 3:15].

Calvary Distinctives

The *entertaining deceptions* within the NAR directly challenge the sound doctrine defined in the Calvary Basics Series, as well as the clear distinctives Pastor Chuck outlined in his book. The rest of this chapter reviews the Calvary Chapel Distinctives and then identifies the "challenge" to each that comes from the false teachings of NAR Apostles, Prophets, churches, and ministries.

1. The Call To Ministry

Pastor Chuck begins that there is a clear call to being in ministry, and that Mark 10:42-44 captures the heart of true pastoral calling. *"Those who are recognized as rulers of the Gentiles lord it over them; and great men exercise authority over them. But it is not this way among you, for whoever wishes to become great among you shall be your servant; and whoever wishes to be first among you shall be slave of all. For even the Son of Man did not come to be served, but to serve, and to give His life a ransom for many"* [p. 9].

THE CHALLENGE - The NAR is more about exalting the individual Apostle or Prophet - the healer, dream interpreter, or one who does signs and wonders. They are built up as spiritually elite and look for the praises of men. But Jesus warned, "They honor themselves as if they were equal to Moses, so then all that they tell you, do not observe it; they place heavy burdens on others, yet do all their deeds to be noticed by men; they love being honored by men and having the choice positions, and being called 'teacher' (or apostle, or prophet) by everyone, but do not be called as such, for you have only teacher, and do not call anyone on earth your spiritual father" [Matthew 23:2-8].

2. God's Model For The Church

Pastor Chuck wrote: "If you look at most church programs today, the chief goal is to add to [numbers attending] the church; [but] you don't have to pay for a seminar to find out how to grow a church, just follow Acts 2:47 and get the people into the Word, prayer, fellowship, and breaking bread, and you'll find the Lord will add to the church daily those that [will] be saved" [p. 16]. And, "the kind of men God used in the church in Acts were totally surrendered to Jesus Christ, not seeking their own glory" [p, 18], whereas "many pastors spend all of their time and energy trying to promote a church, or themselves, but true promotion comes from the Lord, so be careful" [p. 19].

THE CHALLENGE - The NAR is all about drawing in large numbers of people to their churches, rallies, concerts, and special events, with the focus on attracting people to sensational displays of signs, wonders, prophetic words, healings, and other miracles "performed" by those who promote themselves – with very little time spent teaching God's Word, "for they will not endure sound doctrine; but *wanting* instead to have their **ears tickled**, they accumulate for themselves teachers in accordance to their own desires" [2nd Timothy 4:3].

3. Church Government

Paul wrote to pastor Timothy in Ephesus [1st Timothy 3] "This is a true saying, if a man desires the office of *"overseer"* (the epi-skope), he desires a good work; he must be blameless, above reproach, respectable, ABLE TO TEACH the Bible, and free from the love of money". Jesus Christ is the head of the church (Calvary Chapel) - not men. The pastor is in submission to the Lord, as are the elders; complementing them are the assisting pastors, and all are ministering to the needs of the people on a daily basis (p. 27]. If a man is not abiding in Christ and instead walking in the flesh, he is disqualified from the position of an *"overseer"*. That same cooperative board of "overseers" is the hallmark of the Calvary Chapel Association and its Leadership Council.

THE CHALLENGE - The NAR is dominated by men and women that are incredibly egotistical, aspiring to be larger-than-life based upon their claims of fantastic, sensational, supernatural signs and wonders — along with trips to heaven and prophetic words of special revelations that often supersede what's clearly taught in God's Word. They have shown they cannot teach the Bible, and many have become millionaires through their ministries. "These things I have applied to myself so that in us you may learn NOT TO EXCEED THAT WHICH IS WRITTEN [in the God's Word], so that no one of you will become arrogant on behalf of one against the other; but some have become arrogant,

131

as though they are not under authority; but I will find out not by the words of those who are arrogant, but their power - [1st Corinthian 4:6 and 18-19].

4. Empowered By The Spirit

Calvary Chapel believes the Holy Spirit provides the power in the life of the believer. For victory over sin and the flesh; we are to walk after the Spirit and not the flesh" (p. 33). This empowering of the Holy Spirit is separate from the indwelling that occurs at conversion. But there are no particular spiritual manifestations that must happen (such as speaking in tongues) to confirm this. Paul wrote, "Not all work miracles, or prophesy; not all speak in tongues or interpret; not all are apostles, prophets, teachers" [1st Corinthians 12:29-30].

THE CHALLENGE - The NAR places a significant premium on those who do sensational signs and wonders as "proof" of some greater measure of God's Holy Spirit - a more complete anointing. The fantastic and supernatural have become what elevates those in the NAR, and draws people to follow them - seeking, hoping, longing for something more in their lives. This opens wide the door for the abuse of the gifts of the Spirit, as well as the thoughts and ideas of men to being viewed as if from God, even "teaching as doctrine those precepts of men" [Mark 7:9]. THE true Apostle John reminds us, "do not believe every spirit, but test the spirits to see whether they are from God, because many false prophets have gone out into the world" [1st John 4:1].

5. Building The Church God's Way

Calvary Chapel has a relaxed and casual style; not a lot of spiritual hype; and pastors are not trying to motivate people through the flesh, or with shouting at the congregation; this stems from a firm belief that if the Lord does not build the house then they are laboring in vain who try to do so (p. 37]. At Calvary Chapel we trust in the Word of God, and teach it, and rely upon it. We don't have to manufacture anything to grow the church. So then with complete confidence that it's God's church (not the pastors), the leadership simply has to be faithful and watch the Lord work. Feed the sheep a solid diet of God's Word and they will reproduce. No church growth program is necessary as healthy sheep invite friends and family to also come and learn the Bible.

THE CHALLENGE - Once again the NAR places great hype and undue pressure on people in their healing rooms and worship services, their schools of supernatural ministry, signs, and wonders — with a major focus on the special anointing of individuals elevated to elite spiritual status above ordinary Christians. These nationally-branded personalities always have to speak some "new" word of prophecy, or reveal "new" SECRETS for prayer, healing, or hearing God in order to stay attractive to seekers. Pastor Chuck notes, "I find that by the time we get through with the Old Testament, the church is hungry for the New Testament; it keeps building every time we go through [the Bible]; you gain and learn so much more, you've been enriched, it never gets old, it never gets stale, it never gets to the place where you need to find some new gimmick, angle, or experience — it's just the Word of God, alive and powerful and it minsters in the Spirit to the people" [p. 43-44].

6. Grace Upon Grace

Calvary Chapel's position is that without the grace of God, none of us would have a chance; we need it in our lives, we need it daily, we're saved by it personally, but we also stand in God's grace [p. 45]. And having received His mercy and grace, the Lord emphasizes our need to then show mercy and grace. We "seek to minister to hurting people — to see them restored, back on their feet, functioning again" [p. 51]. The grace of God is given to those who have turned from and repented of their sin, and put their faith in Jesus who literally took the price for our sin when He died on the cross. That's a free gift.

THE CHALLENGE - The NAR teaches the deception that God's plan all along was that He was missing us up in heaven, so He made a plan to bring us back to be there with Him. But that's not the Gospel at all. In fact, man was NOT originally with God in heaven - that's God's domain, and He created the earth for mankind. NAR Apostle Todd White told TBN, "The cross doesn't just reveal my sin, it also reveals my value; something underneath my sin must have been of great value for heaven to go bankrupt to get me back". But the NAR has it backwards because it was our SIN that was so great that God provided a Savior - it was not the great value of a man. Galatians 1:6 says "*I am amazed that you are so quickly deserting Him who called you by the grace of Christ, for a different gospel; which is really not another; only there are some who are disturbing you and want to distort the gospel of Christ*".

7. The Priority Of The Word

When Paul met with the elders in Ephesus he said, "I did not hold back teaching you the full counsel of God" [Acts 20:27]. The only way he could make that claim is if he taught through the whole Word of God with them [p. 55]. Pastor Chuck notes that Calvary Chapel is committed to declaring to the people the complete counsel of the Bible. The teaching ministry is expositional in style, as we seek to follow Isaiah 28:13. "So the word of the LORD to them will be, order on order, precept upon precept, line upon line, a little here, a little there". Calvary Chapel is about taking people deeply into a full understanding of God's Word - not listening to men and women recount their own highly sensational personal experiences. In Nehemiah, the leaders gathered the people and built a platform, and starting each morning they read the Word of God to the people - "they read it distinctly, gave the sense, and caused them to understand". That is the heart of expository teaching from the Bible: read it, give the people a solid sense of its meaning, and then they understand it well.

THE CHALLENGE - The NAR teaches very little from God's Word as their apostles, pastors, prophets, and anointed miracle workers rely heavily on their own personal "spiritual" experiences in their podcasts, videos, and books.

8. The Centrality Of Jesus Christ

Calvary Chapel desires that the time in worship, and time in God's Word be free from distractions so the attention remains on Jesus. If someone stands up and starts speaking, dancing, or moving about during the worship service or when the Bible is taught, everyone turns their attention there. It's the same for worship leaders. People should not be focused on them, how the instruments are played, moving around on stage, or words spoken, as these distract people from focusing on Jesus. At Calvary Costa Mesa, if someone stands up during the service, our ushers gently escort them to the foyer and explain, "We don't practice this because we find it draws people's attention away from worship, and surely you wouldn't want that?" [p. 62]. Jesus said to not show your alms before men to be seen of them, otherwise you have no reward of your Father in heaven [Matthew 6:1]. We're also careful about 'strange fire' - emotions that don't originate with God (but with men); drawing attention to men rather than God [p. 67]. In summary, "We need to be cautious about creating an aura around ourselves, loving the adoration from people, because God doesn't want to share His glory; we want Jesus Christ as the focus of our worship" [p.68].

THE CHALLENGE - NAR worship services are the exact opposite, as the focus is entirely on the healer, prophet, apostle, or worship leader and all the signs and wonders THEY do. The line-up of personalities from Chapter-7 have all worked hard to build their name-brand recognition as "God's anointed" - even going so far as the comments through Mike Bickle and Bob Jones that the original 12 Apostles chosen by Jesus are so excited to shake the hands of today's latter rain, third wave Apostles when they get to heaven, because this current group does far more for the kingdom than the original 12 Apostles.

9. The Rapture Of The Church

Pastor Chuck said it well: "The are many people who claim an ignorance of the rapture or say they are uncertain whether it will precede the tribulation; I don't believe there is any excuse for not having a position on this" [p. 69]. Jesus promised, "Let not your heart be troubled, you believe in God believe also in Me; in my Father's house are many mansions - if I go and prepare a place for you I will come again and receive you to Myself that where I am, you may be also" [John 14:1-3]. Pastor Chuck devoted the longest chapter (by more than twice the coverage) explaining dozens of Bible passages that all confirm the pre-tribulation rapture of the church. Calvary believes the literal interpretation of these Scripture verses as the event that sets the stage for revealing of the Antichrist and God's judgment of sin on the earth, both leading up to the

Second Coming of Jesus, when He will rule a literal kingdom in Jerusalem seated on David's throne. This is that "blessed hope" Paul spoke of [Titus 2:13], the "mystery, that we shall not all die, but some will be translated in the time it takes to blink an eye" [1st Corinthians 15]. The rapture is truly a foundational distinctive of Calvary Chapel, and is not a minor point to address casually.

THE CHALLENGE - The NAR is built on replacement theology. As such, they do not believe in the imminent rapture of the church, the millennium is only figurative (not literal), and when the Lord's Prayer says "Thy kingdom come", that has either already been fulfilled in the church age (the a-millennial view), or is set to happen once the church (the bride) is made pure and ready for Jesus to come for her. Many in the NAR also hold to the Preterist position that all of the end-times Bible prophecy in Revelation and other Old Testament books was completed up through Rome's destruction of Jerusalem in 70 A.D.

10. Having Begun In The Spirit

Pastor Chuck recognized, "we are not sufficient (adequate) of ourselves to think anything as of ourselves, but our sufficiency is of God, Who made us able ministers of the new covenant - not of the letter, but of the Spirit, for the letter kills, but the Spirit gives life" [2nd Corinthians 3:5-6]. Calvary Chapel is a movement begun by the Holy Spirit, and it should not try to transition to a place where it will somehow be continued or finalized through the plans of men and their own ideas for church growth. Instead, "God chooses unqualified people, fills them by His Spirit, and then does His mighty work through them" [p. 105]. It is important to simply teach the Word and watch how the Holy Spirit leads.

THE CHALLENGE - The NAR is rooted in the church growth plans of C. Peter Wagner - that miraculous signs and sensational wonders would then anoint the Manifest Sons of God for kingdom-now dominion to subdue the earth and bring heaven down to earth. The Latter Rain (Third Wave), Joel's Army, and accompanying Bridal Eschatology are then the framework for man's plans to grow the church using modern day Apostles and Prophets who will lead and coordinate a single "true" church entirely under their authority.

11. The Supremacy of Love

Calvary Chapel believes that 1st Corinthians 13 provides a strong basis for church life, because even if people have the ability to speak in tongues, or to prophesy, or know all mysteries, and have faith to do amazing wonders, but they don't have true love from God, then all their sensational words and signs are meaningless. "How many times do you read in the Scriptures, 'And Jesus was moved with compassion' when He saw the needs of the people?" [p, 112]. It is important that all we do and say at Calvary is guided by love, which is a fruit of the Holy Spirit - it's not something we have on our own. We are in ministry to show the love of Jesus to others, and always to show people how to give Him glory. We are not in the ministry to bring glory and adoration to ourselves.

THE CHALLENGE - Once again the NAR does not line-up with this distinctive of Calvary Chapel. NAR videos, podcasts, DVDs, books, articles, sermons, MP3s, CDs, and events are not originating from a love for people and compassion on them in their need for a Savior. The focus remains on how super spiritual the anointed personalities are, and the sensational signs, wonders, and miracles they speak of from their personal experiences – and that these same experiences are what people should be seeking after.

12. Striking The Balance

An important characteristic of Calvary Chapel fellowships is that "we don't take a typical Pentecostal view, nor a typical Baptist view, (so) while we believe in the validity of the gifts of the Spirit, we don't believe in the excesses that so often accompany people's use of the gifts; we need to do all things decently and in order" [p.113-115]. Another example is in the debate between Calvinism and Arminianism, where Pastor Chuck has clearly shown that the Bible teaches both – man has free will, yet God already knows those choices because He exists outside of time-space and knows the end from the beginning. So that "as you minister, as you go through the Word of God, you will come across those Scriptures that speak of the sovereignty of God – when you do, teach it;

[and] when you come across the responsibility of man, teach that; in this way you can be sure of feeding the people a well-balanced spiritual diet" [p. 120].

THE CHALLENGE - The NAR is steeped in a hyper-charismatic form of Pentecostalism that is overly focused on sensational displays of miracles, signs, wonders, and prophetic words to draw people into their services, media, and other special events. Not only does this lack balance, but it also leans way too far over into requiring supernatural spiritual manifestations as the only way to know God or confirm that He's truly working in someone's life.

13. Ventures Of Faith

Calvary Chapel believes that when we step out in faith there must be a guard in place against presumption, because people make a serious mistake by falling back on human effort when God is obviously not in it; we get committed to something that puts our reputation on the line and can start putting all kinds of energy and effort into a program that wasn't of God to begin with [p. 121]. Pastor Chuck tells of simply waiting on the Lord about the purchase price for radio station KWVE, "Well Lord, if you want it, fine, and if not, that's fine too" — and they accepted that only offer made. Same for buying property for the Bible college, first in Vista (the Lord closed that door), and then in Murrietta (the Lord opened wide that door). No pressure, anxiety, or stress, and no relying on the efforts of men to make it happen. We all know Pastor Chuck's favorite story about shopping for a new car, finding a great deal, and then simply waiting a day or two to pray over it, confident that "if the Lord wants me to have that car, it'll still be there at that price tomorrow". I remember in the mid-1980s how the Daniel Amos Band started the Monday night outreaches in the Costa Mesa main sanctuary with music and a study in Revelation of the Four Horsemen; then Chuck invited Greg Laurie to lead that study. Lots of young people started coming forward each week to receive Jesus, so they looked into renting the Pacific Amphitheater at the Orange County Fairgrounds to hold more youth, and God opened the door for an entire week, and that was the start of the Harvest Crusades. These and many other testimonies were always summed up in Chuck's principle: 'Where God Guides, God Provides".

THE CHALLENGE - One of the main components of the NAR is the "word-of-faith" doctrine that requires God to do for you whatever you believe Him for. The full range of NAR prophecies, words of knowledge, visions of future events, and "God told me in a dream" absolutely put the person's entire reputation on the line as everyone watches and waits for a miracle or fulfillment. Fantastic claims about world events, sensational words that supposedly come right from God, and public declarations that God WILL do a certain action, each have some sort of "faith" being put to the test, but so much of what the false Apostles and Prophets do and say was never of God in the first place.

Additional Basics

Before Chuck's book on Calvary's distinctives, he was the editor of the *Calvary Basics Series* (1995-1996) and prefaced each book with, "We seem to be living in a day of spiritual confusion [many are] tossed to and fro with every wind of doctrine, [so] we felt it good to have books address these issues and give you the solid biblical basis of what we believe and why we believe it". What a timely word, considering these were published over 20 years ago. I and my pastor Ricky Ryan reviewed four years of my teaching notes from the Calvary Santa Barbara monthly musicians' fellowship and turned those into the book - *Worship And Music Ministry* in this 'Basics' series. The other titles include:

- *Creation By Design* (Dr. Mark Eastman)   - *The Afterglow* (Harold Gainey)
- *Building Godly Character* (Ray Bentley)   - *Christian Leadership* (Larry Taylor)
- *Spiritual Warfare* (Brian Brodersen)   - *The Final Curtain* (Chuck Smith)
- *Practical Christian Living* (Wayne Taylor) - *Enjoying Bible Study* (Skip Heitzig)
- *Answers For The Skeptic* (Scott Richards)
- *The Psychologizing Of The Faith* (Bob Hoekstra)

Calvary Chapel is certainly clear and on-the-record regarding its distinct beliefs. The next chapter covers the Biblical role of overseers - those men responsible for the leadership, protection, and pastoral care of the church.

CHAPTER NINE
The Role Of Calvary Overseers

Pastors And Elders

Paul's first letter to Timothy covered very clear principles about church leadership and administration for that young pastor in the newly planted church at Ephesus. He opened the third chapter, "It is a trustworthy statement - if any man aspires to the office of overseer, it is a fine work he desires". Paul uses the Greek term "epi-skope" (ἐπι σκοπή) meaning "over" (epi) "seer" (skope) - the same root used in periscope, telescope, microscopic, and arthroscopic. It's also the term from 1st Peter 2:25 that describes Jesus as an overseer of the sheep in the church. It's very interesting that "pastor" is the same word in Greek for shepherd ("poimen"), because he both feeds AND tends/cares for (watches over) the sheep - he cannot do one and not the other. Pastor Chuck time and again used his classic saying that "healthy sheep always reproduce", so his focus was to ensure that his sheep at Calvary Costa Mesa were very well fed on God's Word (and we were). Pastor Ricky Ryan always emphasized that the role of the pastor-shepherd is to feed and equip the sheep so they could do the ministry of the church. But sheep tend to wander unless they are led by the shepherd in a specific direction. Jesus regularly uses this analogy to describe the church as sheep, and His role as the Good Shepherd. The sheep hear His voice, know Him, and should not follow the voice of a stranger. A hired sheep-tender has no vested interest in the sheep so that when they are threatened by attack - because he's just a hireling - he flees. But the shepherd loves His own sheep, and always defends them. If even one sheep strays, He will go and find that one and carry it back to the sheepfold. The shepherd watches over the sheep, yet Jesus made clear there would be wolves (false teachers) coming into the sheepfold (the church) disguised to look like sheep, but their only intention is to kill and devour, and scatter the entire flock [Matthew 7:15, Acts 20:29].

So then, pastors and elders (as "overseers") are responsible for the sheep God has placed in their care. Paul explains to Timothy that an overseer must have these 15 characteristics, being: 1) above reproach, 2) the husband of one wife, 3) temperate, 4) prudent, 5) respectable, 6) hospitable, 7) able to effectively teach God's Word, 8) not addicted to wine or 9) pugnacious, but 10) gentle, 11) peaceable, and 12) free from the love of money, and 13) one who manages his own household well, and he's 14) not a new believer in Jesus, so he won't become conceited and fall into "the condemnation incurred by the devil". Finally, 15) of good reputation with all those OUTSIDE the church (that's very interesting), so that he will not fall into reproach and the snare of the devil. Those are significant job requirements. The reason the bar is set so high is because the stakes are equally high. Ordinary, everyday people coming to Calvary Chapel rely on the leadership to provide a trusted and reliable filter - through God's Word and strong spiritual discernment - to ensure that every facet of ministry happening at that particular church is Biblically sound.

Spiritual Discernment Needed

Whenever any kind of false teachers or doctrines show up at the door of the church (or are already inside), it's the responsibility of pastors and elders to be that first line of defense. This only happens when there's clear and consistent spiritual discernment from the Holy Spirit, speaking to the overseers that something's not right. 1st Timothy 1 explains that Paul entrusted Timothy as the pastor in Ephesus to *"fight the good fight, and to keep the faith with a good conscience, which some have rejected and as a result have suffered shipwreck in regard to their faith"*. Paul continued that Timothy and the Ephesian congregation would then *"know how to conduct yourselves in the household of God, which is the church of the living God, the pillar and support of truth"*. It is a good reminder to realize that people in the early church were just as susceptible to wandering off course and damaging their faith, and also needed to be admonished in how to conduct themselves within the church.

It is absolutely the duty of the senior pastor and the elder board to be the primary initiators of alerting the church about the various kinds of deceptive teachings, people, and movements that could influence them. It's important to be pro-active in addressing these issues BEFORE deception shows up in the women's fellowship, youth ministries, worship team, or home Bible studies. Given the NAR's deception being so pervasive in all kinds of books, CDs, DVDs, podcasts, conferences, special events, and websites, it is incumbent upon church leadership to get out in front of these trends and take time to educate their local Calvary congregation from top to bottom. This starts with the senior pastor and his elder board, then moves through the assistant pastors, the church staff, the deacons, and all other lay people who serve as leaders in men's ministry, women's ministry, the Sunday school teachers and volunteers in youth groups and college ministry, the worship leaders and each musician, the counseling and prayer teams, and right on through to the home Bible study teachers, and all those involved in outreach and missions.

Stay In God's Word

In chapter 4 of 1st Timothy, Paul continues to alert Christians that the Holy Spirit explicitly says that *"in succeeding seasons* (the future years of the church) there will be MANY DEPARTING from the faith, paying attention instead to DECEITFUL SPIRITS and DOCTRINE OF DEMONS, by means of the HYPOCRISY

OF LIARS who have been seared in their own conscience as with a branding iron, [so] that in pointing out these things to the brethren, you will be a good servant of Christ Jesus, constantly nourished on the words of the faith and of the SOUND DOCTRINE which you have been following". "Prescribe and TEACH THESE THINGS in all your speech, conduct, love, faith, purity so as to be an example of those who believe, and give attention to the public reading of Scripture, to exhortation, and teaching from God's Word".

Paul concludes his exhortation in chapter 6 that "If anyone advocates a DIFFERENT DOCTRINE and does not agree with sound words, he is conceited and understands nothing; but has a morbid interest in controversial questions and disputes, out of which arise envy, strife, abusive language, evil suspicions, and constant friction between men of depraved mind – who are deprived of the truth - who suppose that godliness is a means of gain". "So guard the Word of God that has been entrusted to you, avoiding worldly and empty chatter, and the opposing arguments of what is falsely being called 'knowledge' - which some have professed and thus GONE ASTRAY from the faith". Did you get that? Many in the church will *depart*, going after *deceitful spirits*, listening to *doctrine of demons*. These are delivered by *lying hypocrites*, who focus on controversial issues, being *deprived of the truth*, and they act so that their form of godliness *can be their means of gain* (things like fame, money, power, attention).

Not If, But When

The challenges coming from NAR false teachers and deceptive doctrines are real and happening as we speak. Calvary Chapel pastors and elders should not wonder IF this might show up at their church, because it's really a matter of WHEN it will show up. Jesus did not say there MIGHT be some wolves trying to get in. He did not say there COULD be a false teacher here or there. God's Word has multiple reminders that "false teachers ARE AMONG YOU, introducing destructive heresies" [2nd Peter 2]. "People will not endure sound teaching, but having itching ears they will get teachers in accordance with their own desires" [2nd Timothy 4]. We are not to believe every spirit, but test whether the spirit is from God, for MANY false prophets are in the world [1st John 4]. False prophets always enter appearing as sheep, but they are ravenous wolves; so you must clearly "distinguish them by their fruit - do you see grapes from bushes, or do figs grow on thistles?" [Matthew 7]. The wolves are 'savage' and will NOT spare the flock [Acts 20]. And Jesus said "I am sending you out as sheep among wolves" [Matthew 10], reminding us that the hired hand is NOT the true Shepherd, so he runs when wolves arrive [John 10]. So for Calvary Chapel leadership, it's clearly not a matter of IF, but WHEN — it's not about how this MIGHT happen, but that it WILL happen (and IS happening).

Tares With Wheat

Perhaps one of the most disturbing and provocative matters about false teachers and spiritual deception in the church is found when Jesus explains the wheat and the tares. In the first portion of Matthew 13, He describes how the Gospel goes out into the world like seed, but lands on different soils (hearts) with various results of acceptance and fruit. He summarizes that with a quote from Isaiah 6:9-10 that people *"Keep on hearing but don't understand, and keep on seeing but don't truly perceive - for the hearts of the people have become dull, their eyes scarcely hear and they have closed their eyes, otherwise they would see and hear, and understand with their hearts, and return to me and I would heal them".* Then Jesus introduces a parable where the enemy of the landowner comes at night to sow weeds in the fields alongside the wheat. As the wheat grows taller, the tares also grew mixed in among the good crop. It was brought to the attention of the master and the servants asked if they should pull out the tares, but the master said, "No, for while you are gathering up the weeds you may also uproot the wheat with them". He gave orders to allow both the wheat and the tares to grow together until the harvest, then HE will use His winnowing fork to separate them, with the wheat being brought into his barns, while the tares are bundled and then burned.

The message is very compelling because we realize that false teachers and other 'wolves in sheep's clothing' WILL in fact be comingled throughout the church. I always wondered why the Lord wouldn't simply do some weeding and get them out of His fields. Talk to any wheat farmer and they'll explain that it takes a highly trained eye to walk chest-deep through wheat fields (not unlike Russell Crowe as Maximus in the film *Gladiator*, arms out to each side gently gliding over the sheaves) and be able to distinguish the stalks of wheat from the various tares that are inevitably woven among them. Jesus used this analogy to explain that now is not the time to do the weeding out - but that winnowing out happens when the Lord comes at His harvest [Matthew 3:12 and Luke 3:17]. Perhaps this is because *"The Lord is not slow about His promise, as some count slowness, but is patient toward [them], not wishing for any to perish but for all to come to repentance"* [2nd Peter 3:9].

It's important to be reminded, that the main reason people are open to look into and pursue these false doctrines, allowing this to grow up right along the good fruit in the church, is because they are not being fed a solid diet of God's Word, so they remain hungry for something else to fill that empty feeling inside, and soon they are watching podcasts, reading books, stopping by the healing rooms, or attending that concert or miracle healing service as a way to try and find what they think is missing in their spiritual experience.

Security Details

It's ironic that many Calvary churches spend so much time, energy, and resources on providing physical security teams to guard the parking lot and facilities from would-be troublemakers - even having men undercover sitting in the front row during services, at the ready to take down anyone who might rush the stage or utter some kind of threat to the pastor or congregation. But the more important questions should be, "Who's on the spiritual wall guarding the church from *entertaining deception* that wants to come in among the people?" It's sad when a Calvary Chapel has the physical location locked down by men on the security detail, yet the wolves in sheep's clothing have easy access to enter in and casually introduce false teaching and spiritual deception without any Biblical security. During the 20 years (1990-2010) that Ricky Ryan was senior pastor at Calvary Chapel Santa Barbara, he called together the elders, pastors, staff, and lay leaders - usually three times a year - for a time to communicate (and get everyone on the same page about) church vision and what's coming up in the life of the church. Elders stood shoulder-to-shoulder as "overseers" with him, charged with feeding, caring for, and protecting the sheep. It seems very appropriate that Calvary pastors and elders should use such a time to be pro-active and inform their churches about the current state of the NAR and the various false teachers and *entertaining deception* happening at this time.

A Summary Charge

To all the pastors and elders in leadership at every Calvary Chapel, hear God's Word regarding your sacred calling and duty within the church. *"Be on guard for yourselves and for all the flock, among which the Holy Spirit has made you overseers, to shepherd the church of God which He purchased with His own blood"* [Acts 20:28]. *"For you know whom you have believed and you are convinced that He is able to guard that which has been entrusted to you, through Him, until that day"* [2ⁿᵈ Timothy 1:12]. *"Therefore, I exhort the elders among you, as your fellow elder and witness of the sufferings of Christ, and a partaker also of the glory that is to be revealed, to shepherd the flock of God among you, exercising oversight not under compulsion, but voluntarily, according to the will of God; and not for sordid gain, but with eagerness; and not lording it over those allotted to your charge, but rather proving to be examples to the flock, so that when the Chief Shepherd appears, you will receive the unfading crown of glory"* [1ˢᵗ Peter 5:1-4]. *"So then beloved, knowing this beforehand, be on your guard so that you are not carried away by the error of unprincipled men and fall from your own steadfastness"* [2ⁿᵈ Peter 3:17]. There is great spiritual responsibility for overseers to be absolutely certain that their eyes remain fixed on Jesus, their hearts ready to hear the Holy Spirit's leading, and with God's Word as the sole basis by which to discern truth from a lie.

In Paul's 2nd letter to Timothy he starts chapter 1 with, "Retain the STANDARD of SOUND WORDS which you have heard from me, in the faith and love which are in Christ Jesus; and GUARD, through the Holy Spirit who dwells in us, THIS TREASURE which has been entrusted to you; the DOCTRINE which you have heard from me in the presence of many witnesses, entrust to faithful men who will be able TO TEACH OTHERS also". In chapter 2 he continues with, "Be DILIGENT to present yourself approved to God as a workman who does not need to be ashamed, ACCURATELY HANDLING THE WORD OF TRUTH, avoiding worldly, empty chatter, that leads to further ungodliness; their kind of talk will spread like gangrene; so be kind to all, ABLE TO TEACH, patient when wronged, with gentleness CORRECTING THOSE who are in opposition". Then in chapter 3 he warns that, "Men will be lovers of self and money; arrogant, conceited; and hold a FORM OF GODLINESS - always learning but never coming to knowledge of the truth. These evil men are IMPOSTERS, proceeding from bad to worse, DECEIVING others while they themselves ARE BRING DECEIVED. You however, continue in the SOUND TEACHINGS you know, because ALL Scripture is God-breathed and profitable for teaching, reproof, correction, and training in righteousness, so that the man of God is ADEQUATELY EQUIPPED for every good work". Paul concludes in Chapter 4, "I solemnly charge you, PREACH THE LOGOS, be ready in season and out, because the time will come when they will not endure sound doctrine; wanting instead to have their ears tickled, they will accumulate for themselves teachers in accordance to their own desires, TURNING AWAY their ears FROM TRUTH and will turn aside to MYTHS".

It's interesting that during the 1970s church leaders made it a point to inform the youth at Calvary Chapel about the dangers of various cults and false religious systems such as the Mormons, Jehovah's Witnesses, Scientology, the Moonies (Unification Church), Hare Krishnas, Christian Science, Self-realization Fellowship, and the like. But today, there is little being said by pastors and elders about the *entertaining deception* subtly coming into Calvary Chapels from the NAR. The ramifications of being lax about *entertaining deception* will have a negative impact on church life. Sad to say, many senior pastors and elders seem to not have the spiritual maturity (backbone) to take a firm stand against those who are bringing NAR beliefs and practices into Calvary ministries. My prayer is that Calvary pastors and elders would be like the church leaders from Ephesus cited by Jesus, "I know your deeds, your work, and perseverance, that you do not tolerate evil men, and YOU PUT TO TEST those who call themselves apostles and they are not, and you found them to be false" [Revelation 2:2].

The closing chapter looks at potential directions still to come for Calvary Chapels, from both the NAR influence, as well as the current issues unfolding between the Calvary Chapel Association and the Calvary Chapel Global Network.

CHAPTER TEN
Potential Directions
Still To Come

Two Reactions

In the first nine chapters we covered sound Biblical doctrine, spiritual deception, the NAR, signs and wonders, God's Word vs. personal experiences, how deception gets into the church, who's out there on the current NAR scene, how the NAR challenges Calvary Chapel distinctives, and the leadership role for overseers. So now what? Over the last ten years I've had many conversations about these same topics, and done many teachings at Calvary Chapels and various men's fellowships, home groups, and pastor's conferences on these critical issues, and there have typically been two reactions that people have.

The first reaction is to dismiss what has been raised as alarmist in tone, maybe a bit nitpicking on too many details that really don't matter, and perhaps you view the book as somewhat negative in judging another's view of the Bible. You might even feel sympathetic toward the NAR, telling yourself, "Hey, they're Christians like me, right? and seem very sincere in their expressions, so who's to say what's right and wrong on these doctrinal disputes". Quite honestly, I've also had people say to me, "Dr. Dave, you really need to step back and chill out about all this" - and I've even been dubbed "the Bible police" by a few guys who think my doctrinal scrutiny takes the wind out of a lot of people's sails who are really into prophetic words, miracles, visions, healings, signs, and wonders.

The second reaction is that people are really surprised about the details of what's going on in this global NAR movement. Many tell me, "Wow, I literally had no idea any of this was happening". Most people come up after my talks and say they could hardly believe the kinds of signs and wonders covered in Chapter-4, or the far-reaching impacts of NAR replacement theology from Chapter-3. Two questions I typically get asked are: "Shouldn't we do something about this to ensure our church is on the right track?" and, "The pastors and elders need to handle this on behalf of the congregation, right?" My responses are always, "Yes" and "Yes". I'll close out the book by looking at some potential directions this *entertaining deception* might take, first on the Micro-Level of an individual church, and then the Macro-Level for all Calvary Chapel churches.

Micro Level

The NAR challenges and negative impacts to Calvary Chapel WILL continue. I fully expect them to increase and become more accepted. Pastors and elder boards must be clear on defining what their church stands for and how they won't compromise sound doctrine. This requires a redoubling of their efforts as overseers across all ministries to ensure that there's consistency of sound doctrine from top to bottom. This is not the time to soften the stand on holding to sound doctrine in order to make church more accessible and seeker-friendly for younger people who are just not into the "old" practices of Biblically sound worship and verse-by-verse expository teaching from God's Word. Pastors in each Calvary need to spend some pulpit time teaching and informing their sheep about what's happening and who are the NAR personalities. Signs and wonders will remain a strong draw for individuals who feel their Christian walk is lacking and needs more spiritual experiences to confirm God at work in them. This will be very similar to the impasse that Pastor Chuck and John Wimber were at 35 years ago, so nothing's "new" about this 'Third Wave' NAR.

Macro Level

The NAR impacts will also happen on the much wider scope of the entire Calvary movement. The three main issues will most likely be: 1) the meaning and use of the "Calvary Chapel" name, 2) affiliations between Calvary Chapels and other churches, ministries, organizations, and 3) changes in key doctrinal positions. The background for these begins with understanding the Calvary Chapel Association (CCA), the CCA Leadership Council, and the "new" Calvary Chapel Global Network (CCGN), and the potential future role of the NAR.

The *CCA and CCGN*

At the 2012 Calvary pastor's conference, Pastor Chuck made clear the Calvary Chapel movement belongs first and foremost to Jesus - who is the Head of he church. Chuck knew that being in his mid-80s it was important to put in place a clear succession mechanism to insure continuity of leadership, vision, and philosophy of ministry after his death. The CCA was the entity for Calvary churches to be affiliated with one another, would oversee the start-up process of new Calvary Chapels, and host pastor's conferences for encouragement and dialogue among all the churches around the world. Chuck invited 19 pastors to serve on the CCA Leadership Council, to ensure that one person would not be able to step in after his passing to assume the sole leadership of the Calvary movement. These men would essentially be an elder board of "epi-skopes" to oversee all the pastors in the Calvary movement, and included men such as Don McClure, Raul Ries, Mike Macintosh, Jeff Johnson, Malcolm Wild, and Jack Hibbs. The following year Chuck penned this July 19, 2013 letter to all Calvary pastors:

> "It seems there are voices being raised and concerns being put forth about the future or direction of our fellowship as Calvary Chapels. I thought it necessary to once more be as clear and deliberate as possible to state my heart in this matter. The Calvary Chapel Association (CCA) are my spiritual sons, men that I love and trust, and have prayerfully asked to embrace the

leadership and influence I believe God has called them to. I am confident they will stay the course, honor my vision for ministry, maintain the Calvary Distinctives, and oversee the affiliation process with the Lord's leading and blessing. This is my heart and theirs. We, together, would ask for the unity of the Spirit and the bond of peace in these things."

Notice the key words in the letter that present no ambiguity about his intention for the CCA going forward. First, there are "CONCERNS being raised about the future direction". Chuck understood that several men were trying to position themselves as the "heir apparent" at Calvary Costa Mesa and the leadership of the overall Calvary Chapel movement, and wanted to take Calvary in a different direction. Second, "I want to be CLEAR and DELIBERATE in communicating my heart on this matter". You can hear Chuck's intent coming through loud and clear directly to the Leadership Council and to all pastors of Calvary churches. Third, "I love and TRUST these men". He was no doubt very confident that these 19 pastors were trustworthy to handle things well after his death. Fourth, "I am CONFIDENT that they will STAY THE COURSE, HONOR MY VISION, and MAINTAIN the Calvary Distinctives as they oversee the CCA". He obviously believed these men understood the future direction to pursue. Fifth, Chuck said he knew this was THEIR HEART like his own, so he believed they were on the same page. And Sixth, he asked for UNITY by the Holy Spirit to keep everyone together in a BOND of PEACE; Chuck did not want a church split. Then three months later, on October 13th, 2013 Pastor Chuck went to be with the Lord.

Fast forward ahead to the 2014 pastor's conference. Brian Brodersen is now the senior pastor at Calvary Costa Mesa, and he invites several younger pastors who were newer to Calvary to speak. They had messages that tended to be somewhat condescending regarding older, longstanding pastors (videos available online). They even spoke openly about Pastor Chuck's failures and how a fresh "new" perspective is needed for today's generation. Then came the main speakers: Sandy Adams [Calvary Chapel Stone Mountain, Georgia], Brian Brodersen, and Wayne Taylor [Calvary Fellowship, Seattle]. This next section in quotations is entirely my own editorial interpretation that summarizes what I watched, read, researched, interviewed others about, and listened to from that conference. Others, no doubt, have different perspectives on what transpired.

[Newton's Summary]: "Pastor Chuck has Calvary Chapels stuck in the past, focused on a depressing message that the world is getting darker, Old Testament prophecy supports that, and all we're doing is waiting for the rapture to remove the church. This is not what younger people want to hear. We need to provide teens, college-age, young professionals, and younger families a way to feel they can do something positive for the kingdom of God, so adjustments are needed in how we teach the Bible so it will be much more relevant for this particular time, culture, and generation".

My initial reply is it's very important to remember that if this younger generation of 'millennials' feels this way, that's not a problem inherent in God's Word losing it's relevancy for them, but rather it's entirely dependent on the pastor's ability to effectively teach (exposit) the Bible with application and clarity. I find it so ironic (and troubling) that their opinions about needing to change how the Bible is taught for today's "unique" situation of younger people completely disregards Calvary Chapel's own history, as Pastor Chuck taught verse-by-verse through God's Word for another "unique" generation and culture of 1960s-1970s hippies in Orange County - and that produced amazing fruit, and was the catalyst that propelled Calvary Chapel to 1,700 churches.

Brian announced to the pastors he would no longer teach through the Bible verse-by-verse as Chuck did, but would move to an "overview model" that covers the books of the Bible across broader themes, to make it more accessible to younger audiences. He even said that being bound or compelled to teach in the same tradition of Chuck could actually be a "form of idolatry". There was some debate as Brian questioned the relevancy of teaching books like Leviticus compared to the Gospel of John, as Sandy replied that the 39 O.T books remain incredibly relevant with amazing foreshadows that shed detailed light and commentary on the 27 New Testament books.

It was very peculiar to me that the conference wrapped up with Alistair Begg speaking on the need for pastor's to have fidelity [no doubt alluding to recent news about a popular Calvary pastor's adultery with several women]. My first concern is why conclude with that topic? Certainly any video from Pastor Chuck's archives about his philosophy of ministry and the Calvary Distinctives would have been much more appropriate for the first pastor's conference after his death. My second concern is why does Brian invite a guy who is not a Calvary pastor, and introduce him as "the most qualified" teacher to conclude the conference? Let me say that I respect Begg's teaching and love for the Lord and God's Word, but he is a longtime member of *The Gospel Coalition* and committed to classic Reformed theology that differs with Calvary Chapel in many areas, including holding to Calvinism, and dispensational theology that does not acknowledge the gifts of the Holy Spirit for today's church.

Perhaps the most obvious take-away from the conference was there was no mention at all of the Calvary distinctives or Pastor Chuck's 2013 letter to the pastors to "stay the course, honor my vision for ministry, and maintain those distinctives". All this, less than a year after Chuck's passing.

What followed the 2014 conference was very disconcerting, and many Calvary pastors still cannot believe how quickly things changed. Brian put in place a series of moves that completely altered the intent of Chuck's 2013 letter. Brian notified all pastors there was "division among the Calvary Chapels" and he would resign from the CCA Leadership Council and unilaterally remove Calvary Costa Mesa from the CCA. Soon after he announced the launch of his "new" Calvary Chapel Global Network (CCGN). He reorganized the Calvary Costa Mesa board, took full editorial control of the CalvaryChapel.com website, and notified all Calvary churches they would need to update their information if they wanted to continue being listed in the church-locator online. Brian contacted all the Calvary churches quoting Amos 3:3 *"can two men walk together unless they agree"* as his rationale for leaving the CCA and starting the CCGN. This created a great deal of confusion, because if there's no major differences between the CCA, it's Leadership Council, the Calvary Distinctives, and Brian's positions for going forward, why would there be a need to create a "new" and entirely separate CCGN? The most logical reason is that Brian wants to have full control going forward to do whatever he wants without being hindered by accountability to the other senior pastors on the CCA Leadership Council.

One other infamous comment from Brian is on the video from the 2016 Northwest pastor's conference, saying he wanted to see pastors "tone it down" with regard to teaching the Old Testament, and "stop beating the drum" about end times prophecy. This was obviously in support of younger, newer Calvary pastors who said that Calvary Chapels are losing hundreds of younger people to churches with a message more tailored to their culture and generation.

Almost 40 years ago, John Wimber and Chuck Smith agreed to part ways to pursue different visions for how Calvary should function. John was catering to the "Emerging Church" that wanted more signs and wonders. Chuck was committed to Calvary's distinctives. The major shift in the Calvary philosophy of ministry with Brian Brodersen is similar to the Calvary-Vineyard divergence from the early 1980s. Pastor Chuck's longstanding vision and distinctives, clearly referred to in his 2013 letter regarding the role of the CCA, were the same held opposite Wimber's preferred "new" direction. And yet Brian Brodersen has positioned himself as the leader for another "new" direction, but this time it's Calvary Chapel (through the main church in Costa Mesa) that will be moving to a different vision and philosophy. Hundreds of Calvary pastors and elder boards now have to decide if they will remain affiliated with Costa Mesa and Brian's CCGN, or stay committed to Pastor Chuck's vision and philosophy of ministry. Once again this is catering to that "Emerging Church" rationale to make CCGN more relevant, connected to, and accepted by a "new" culture and generation.

In November 2016, the CCA Leadership Council sent its own letter to all Calvary Chapels (the complete text is available online). The highlights were:

- *CCGN "now threatens the legacy" of Chuck's vision*
- *CCGN will "de-emphasize our Calvary distinctives"*
- *CCGN "establishes a different vision and will cause confusion"*
- *"Brian claims authority to represent and define what Calvary is"*

- *This division "is not a minor issue"*
- *Brian has "sole editorial control of CalvaryChapel.com" and states "this explains the theological positions held" [by all Calvary]*
- *Brian [unilaterally moved] the CCA into his own network*
- *"Calvary is built on the foundations from Pastor Chuck" but CCGN is a blueprint devised by [one man] Brian"*

- *"CCA is led by a group of men, CCGN is directed by one man"*
- *"CCA has a philosophy of ministry, CCGN has no formal affiliation"*
- *"CCA has regional emphasis, CCGN is centralized in Costa Mesa"*
- *"CCA has always afforded freedom [for churches] with accountability CCGN has freedom with no accountability"*

The letter wrapped up with: *"we will not be part of Brian's CCGN"* and in spite of the dark clouds hanging over Calvary Chapel during this time of division, *"our vision is clearer and the future is brighter"*. Quite a turn of events, all within a very short time after Pastor Chuck's death. It certainly treads right on his 2013 letter that said: *"I am confident they will stay the course, honor my vision for ministry, maintain the Calvary Distinctives, [and] this is my heart and theirs"*

Brian's "new" leadership has decided to NOT stay the course, to NOT honor his father-in-law's vision, and NOT maintain the Calvary Distinctives and affiliation process. This clearly shows he did NOT share the same heart Chuck wrote of.

The NAR-Calvary Future

It's important to remember that the NAR does not function like Calvary. The term "New Apostolic Reformation" is not a church or ministry organization. It is a philosophy of ministry embracing false doctrines built on replacement theology with an emphasis on signs, wonders, miracles, and prophetic words that do not line up with God's Word. There's no NAR home church from which other NAR churches are launched, and there's no official NAR named affiliation among various churches and ministries. Rather, the NAR is a global movement that includes multiple churches and denominations that all *entertain deception* on the broader principles discussed in Chapter-3, and the various signs and wonders from Chapter-4. Moving away from the Calvary distinctives while centralizing authority under Brian Brodersen has positioned the CCGN to pursue "other" non-Calvary NAR affiliations, alliances, and partnerships. Potential "new" things coming in the future for the CCGN could include: 1) formal cooperation with global organizations that hold to kingdom-now dominionism and other NAR false teachings, 2) CCGN worship conferences/concerts with Hillsong and Bethel Music/Jesus Culture musicians, 3) evangelism and outreach events that will have well-known NAR Apostles and Prophets alongside CCGN pastors, 4) KWVE radio giving airtime to Hillsong and Bethel/Jesus Culture worship music with their *entertainingly deceptive* lyrics that promote false doctrines, 5) KWVE programs will have more non-Calvary Chapel pastors in the teaching line-up [NOTE: Mrs. Willie Jordan from LA Rescue Mission, Alistair Begg, Eric Buehrer of Gateways, and Rick Warren of Saddleback Church already have regular KWVE programs], 6) NAR personalities will co-author "new" books with Brian and other CCGN pastors, and 7) NAR personalities will be guests on KWVE programs. It is also likely that women will begin to teach more and more from the pulpit at Calvary Costa Mesa, and in time the issue of "female pastors" will be openly discussed, all in the direction of eventually having women be CCGN pastors and teach [NOTE: Sarah Yardley taught at the 2016 Calvary Missions Conference in Costa Mesa]. This will position CCGN more closely with "Emerging Church" and husband-wife co-pastors like Brian and Bobbie Houston, Bill and Beni Johnson, John and Carol Arnott, and many others throughout the NAR.

The "Calvary Chapel" Name

Alongside the doctrinal and philosophy-of-ministry concerns, the name of "Calvary Chapel" is going to be a major issue with potentially far-reaching ramifications on both sides of this divergence. The "Calvary Chapel" name represents a significant intellectual property (IP) asset with 50 years of goodwill embedded in its value to churches. But implicit connotations of "Calvary Chapel" are going to change dramatically the further Brian moves CCGN away from the Calvary distinctives and into "new" alliances and affiliations with other NAR-influenced organizations, ministries, and churches around the world. The value and leveraging of IP are crucial for the strategic positioning of organizations. A colleague of mine is a high-level business attorney and we both agree that it is very probable that the "Calvary Chapel" name will become a major issue on the Macro-Level for the CCA, the CCGN, and all Calvary Chapel churches. Here's what could happen. While Calvary Costa Mesa and the CCGN move further into NAR influenced affiliations, the CCGN could eventually claim that the "Calvary Chapel" name can only be used by them and their approved ministry and alliances in their global network. They could seek an injunction against all non-CCGN Calvary Chapels from using "their" name. In essence, they would try to make the case that Calvary Costa Mesa owns that brand name and unless a church is in the CCGN, it cannot infringe on that IP asset. This could force non-CCGN Calvary Chapels to rename their church, and the same could happen with the CCA, forcing it to drop "Calvary Chapel" from its title. Fifty years of strong, positive goodwill have accrued within the Calvary Chapel brand name. Can the CCA hold onto and further strengthen that brand of excellence, or will mixed messages force a competition issue between the CCA and the CCGN?

Men Can Get It Wrong

It is very troubling that the same issues and concerns are no longer isolated instances occurring at one, or just a few, Calvary Chapels. Instead, the full range of NAR deception is showing up at a LOT of Calvary Chapel churches. One of the most common things to hear is: "The worship at our church has really changed and we're no longer comfortable with what's happening, so we skip the 30 minutes of worship at the start of the service and arrive later for the teaching". Another is: "Well, a large number of us parents have many times spoken with our senior pastor about our concerns with what's going on in the high school group, but he has not really done anything, and meanwhile it just keeps getting worse, so our teenagers no longer attend". I have also heard: "The primary focus and activity of our men's fellowship is no longer a deep Bible study, instead we spend our time listening to guys share their personal experiences about the supernatural ways that God is manifesting Himself in their lives", and "We used to be very active in a home Bible study, but lately it's been focused on reading the latest books on healing or miracles, discussing these, and then waiting on the Lord to display supernatural signs and wonders".

Fold in the events unfolding across the Calvary Chapel movement, and the negative impacts of the NAR on many Calvary Chapel churches, and these simply show once again that men are fallible - and when their eyes get turned aside from the sound doctrine of God's Word, they can absolutely get it wrong. This applies to the NAR Apostles and Prophets, and their "precepts of men" taught as if they were doctrine. This applies to Calvary Chapel pastors or elders who neglect their responsibilities as overseers and allow NAR false teachings to enter in. And it applies to the precarious direction in which Brian Brodersen has set a course for his "new" vision of the CCGN. The months and years ahead will be a very interesting time regarding the degree to which NAR false teachings and deceptions could become more involved in church life at various Calvary Chapels. It will also be important to see how far Brian takes the CCGN into formal legal partnerships with various NAR influenced individuals and their churches, ministries, and organizations, as he increasingly looks outside Calvary Chapel to build affiliations for his global network.

I'd like to think that the CCGN will ultimately end up being only about 100 or so Calvary Chapels aligned with Brian's "new" roadmap, while some 1,600 Calvary Chapels will strengthen the CCA as THE most prominent and recognized "Calvary" name - built on sound doctrine, the Calvary distinctives, and the vision and philosophy of ministry of Pastor Chuck. May we all honor the Lord, as well as Chuck's legacy with "unity of the Spirit and a bond of peace" as the CCA takes an organization- and church-wide stand against the very real challenges to sound doctrine from the *entertaining deception* of the NAR.

APPENDIX

The following resources provide additional research and commentary on the NAR's *entertaining deception*. With nods to T. A. McMahon and *Berean Call Ministries* co-founder - the late Dave Hunt - as well as to Chuck Missler at *Koinonia House*, my strong desire is that you will be just like those Christians noted in Acts 17:11, who were more noble-minded, astute, apt to think more deeply, because not only were they eager to receive the Word, but they searched the Scriptures daily to see if in fact what the Apostle Paul had taught them was true. Everyone can and must be diligent and discerning as the NAR continues to make advances into the mission and ministry of Calvary Chapel.

BOOKS
A New Apostolic Reformation? A Biblical Response To A Worldwide Movement, R Douglas Gievett and Holly Pivec (Weaver Books, 2014)

The New Apostolic Reformation: History Of A Modern Charismatic Movement, John Weaver (McFarland & Company, 2016)

The New Reformation: What Is It And Where Is It Going? Sandy Simpson (Apologetics Coordination Team Publishing, 2004)

The *New Reformation: An Assessment Of The New Apostolic Reformation From Toronto To Redding,* Frederick Osborn (Creative Publishing, 2016)

ⓘ

Deception In The Church: The New Apostolic Reformation And The Emergent Church, Mumbi Kariuki (2016).

ⓘ

God's Super Apostles: Encountering The Worldwide Prophets And Apostles Movement , R. Douglas Gievett and Holly Pivec (Weaver Books, 2014)

ⓘ

Kundalini Warning: Are False Spirits Invading The Church?, Andrew Strom (Revival School Publishers, 2010).

ⓘ

Strange Fire: The Danger Of Offending The Holy Spirit With False Worship, John MacArthur (2013).

ⓘ

Why I Left The Prophetic Movement, Andrew Strom (Revival School, 2007).

ⓘ

Worship And Music Ministry , Ricky Ryan and Dave Newton (The Calvary Basics Series from The Word For Today, 1994 – Chuck Smith, General Editor).

ⓘ

DVD SERIES

Wide Is The Gate: The Emerging New Christianity, Chris Qunitana, Senior Pastor, Calvary Chapel Cypress (available at Amazon.com)

OUR WEBSITE

NewtonInsightsNAR.org — Research summaries and links to our partners, how to buy the book, and more information related to Calvary and the NAR.

OTHER WEBSITES

ApologeticsCoordinationTeam (ACT) and *Moriel Ministries Int'l* — Research articles, commentary, reviews on the NAR. Editor: Sandy Simpson

ⓘ

ApologeticsIndex.org — Research summaries, editorial papers, books, and commentary on the NAR. Founded by: Anton Hein.

ⓘ

TheBereanCall.org — Detailed research articles, books, videos and editorial commentaries on the NAR. Editors: TA McMahon and the late Dave Hunt.

ⓘ

BereanResearch.org — Numerous white papers, research summaries, and editorial commentaries on the NAR. Editors: Amy Spreeman, Marsha West.

ⓘ

CARM.org — Christian Apologetics Research Ministry has numerous articles and links to podcasts and websites dealing with false doctrines and the NAR.

ⓘ

DeceptionInTheChurch.com — Developed by the Apologetics Coordination Team (ACT), has dozens of position papers dealing with a wide variety of NAR related topics from various researcher-authors.

HealthyLeaders.com — Posts articles by various authors that examine the lack of mature spiritual leadership in many of the "new" emerging churches.

ⓘ

LighthouseTrailsResearch.com — Provides sound primary research and commentary on NAR trends and practices in the contemporary church.

ⓘ

TheNarrowingPath.com — Australian based apologetics team researching false doctrines and the NAR. Sponsored by: Trinity Community Church.

ⓘ

OnePlace.com/UnderstandingTheTimes — Research, editorial articles, and Biblical commentaries on the NAR. Editor: Jan Markell.

ⓘ

PirateChristian.com — Christ-centered and Cross-focused radio program with commentary-articles on the NAR. Editor: Chris Rosebrough.

ⓘ

SpiritOfError.org — Numerous white papers, research summaries, and editorial commentaries on the NAR. Editor: Holly Pivec.

ⓘ

StandUpForTruth.com — Radio show and research-review of emerging trends in churches, including the NAR. Editors: Mike LeMay, David Fiorazo.

About The Author

Dr. Newton has been active in Calvary Chapel since 1984, and has seen first-hand the impact Pastor Chuck has had on introducing people to Christ and growing them up in their understanding of God's Word. He has a deep heartfelt affection for the ministry of Pastor Chuck, and wants to see Calvary Chapels everywhere continue in a solid commitment to the core *Calvary Distinctives*. In 1981, Dave started listening to "The Word For Today" on WEZE while an MBA student in Boston. In 1984 he and his wife Kim moved to Orange County and he started teaching finance at the Pepperdine MBA program in Irvine. They attended Calvary Costa Mesa's Sunday 9:30am service, as well as Sunday night and Thursday evening Bible studies with Chuck. She was a small group leader in Joyful Life Thursday mornings with Kay Smith, and Dave went to the musicians fellowship organized by John Wickham, Oden Fong, and Darrell Mansfield - and the Saturday morning For Men Only (FMO) fellowship. He also attended Monday evenings to hear Chuck Missler in the Fellowship Hall. They went on men's and women's retreats at Twin Peaks, and family camps with their kids each summer. Dave played in an '80s new wave Christian outreach band with guys from Calvary, and helped start a home Bible study that met weekly from 1984-1990. Three of their four children were born in Orange County, and they have fond memories of each being dedicated to the Lord by Pastor Chuck. In 1990 they moved north and plugged in at Calvary Chapel Santa Barbara, which had just picked up a new pastor - Ricky Ryan from Mau'i - with an assist from Pastor Chuck. During Ricky's 20 years at CCSB (1990-2010), Dave was a worship leader (1990-2000), taught the musicians' fellowship, and co-authored with Ricky *Worship And Music Ministry* in the Calvary Basics Series. He taught children's Sunday school, adults at Twin Peaks family camps each summer, and launched the Santa Barbara extension of Calvary Chapel Bible College. Dr. Newton served on the elder board for 5 years, and taught from the pulpit regularly when Pastor Ricky was away. His teaching of God's Word also included 9 years leading the men's "Figure It Out" Bible study, being one of the speakers at the annual Central Coast Prophecy Conference (with Ricky, Jack Hibbs, Lance Ralston, and others), and in 2016 he taught a Tuesday evening study on End Times Bible Prophecy. Dr. Dave has taught many times at Calvary Chapels in East London (Docklands), Nice and Lyon (France), the European Calvary pastors' conference in Siegen, and the Calvary Scandinavian conference near Stockholm. He was a full-time college professor for 28 years, and since 2012, he now consults, writes, speaks, and teaches two days a month with the Center for Executive Development in the Rady School of Management at UCSD.